CAN SCIENCE EXPLAIN RELIGION?

Can Science
Explain Religion?

The Cognitive Science Debate

James W. Jones

OXFORD
UNIVERSITY PRESS

OXFORD
UNIVERSITY PRESS

Oxford University Press is a department of the University of
Oxford. It furthers the University's objective of excellence in research,
scholarship, and education by publishing worldwide.

Oxford   New York
Auckland   Cape Town   Dar es Salaam   Hong Kong   Karachi
Kuala Lumpur   Madrid   Melbourne   Mexico City   Nairobi
New Delhi   Shanghai   Taipei   Toronto

With offices in
Argentina   Austria   Brazil   Chile   Czech Republic   France   Greece
Guatemala   Hungary   Italy   Japan   Poland   Portugal   Singapore
South Korea   Switzerland   Thailand   Turkey   Ukraine   Vietnam

Oxford is a registered trademark of Oxford University Press
in the UK and certain other countries.

Published in the United States of America by
Oxford University Press
198 Madison Avenue, New York, NY 10016

Library of Congress Cataloging-in-Publication Data
Jones, James William, 1943-
Can science explain religion? : the cognitive science debate / James W. Jones.
pages cm
Includes bibliographical references and index.
ISBN 978-0-19-024938-0 (cloth : alk. paper)
1. Religion and science.   I. Title.
BL240.3.J66 2015
201'.65—dc23
2015005056

1 3 5 7 9 8 6 4 2
Printed in the United States of America
on acid-free paper

CONTENTS

ACKNOWLEDGMENTS

This book was conceived and written while I was a visiting research fellow in the Psychology of Religion Research Group at Cambridge University in the United Kingdom. I am deeply grateful to Doctor Fraser Watts, the group's director, for the invitation to spend a year working there, and to Leon Turner and Ryan Williams, two of my colleagues in that group, for continual conversations about psychological research and the role of cognitive science, and for reading and providing detailed criticisms of an earlier draft. I am also deeply grateful to Professor Sarah Coakley, for graciously inviting me to participate in various graduate theology and philosophy seminars in the Cambridge Divinity Faculty and for the opportunity to discuss her forthcoming Gifford Lectures and other topics at the interface of science and religion. Dr. Watts and Professor Coakley allowed me to attend their courses of lectures: his on theology and science, and on theology and psychology; hers on philosophy of religion. They both organized a seminar for faculty and graduate students for me to present this material, at which it received a thorough and critical review. The manuscript is much clearer and stronger for that experience. Thanks also to Rodney Holder, Kelley Bulkeley, Sara Savage, Timothy Jenkins, and Denis Alexander for their comments and criticisms. I am immensely grateful for the critical work and strong encouragement from these colleagues in psychology, philosophical theology, sociology, physics, and biology. In addition, Rodney and Shirley Holder graciously welcomed me to Cambridge and facilitated the honor of being admitted to St. Edmund's College as a Visiting Fellow. Dr. Watts and Professor Coakley and the members of the Psychology of Religion Research Group and the Divinity Faculty theology seminars extended a gracious hand of collegiality and immersed me in world of intensely sophisticated reflection on topics related to this project. My dear friend Peter Selby was there in London to provide needed friendship, travel information, and discussion of the broader implications of the work I was doing.

This work was supported in part by a grant from the John Templeton Foundation. The opinions expressed here are those of the author and do not necessarily reflect the views of the John Templeton Foundation. Nick Gibson, my contact there, went above and beyond the call of duty helping me prepare this grant. Rutgers University provided a sabbatical leave for the time I spent in Cambridge. The Rutgers University Research Council provided a small grant to help with conference attendance to report my findings. Joe Broderick and his colleagues in various university grants departments helped me through the maze of grant applications and administration. I am grateful for the suggestions of several anonymous reviewers, which greatly strengthened the argument of this book. Judy Goldman provided first-rate editing and proofreading assistance with the final version. And, as always, Cynthia Read was a supportive, gracious, and masterful editor.

The presence of Kathleen Bishop, my life-time companion in love and work, enables me, in the language of D. W. Winnicott, to go on being. In gratitude for that, no words are possible.

NOTE ON SOURCES

Since this book is written for general readers I have not laden the text with footnotes or references. At the end is an appendix, where research and arguments supporting what I say can be found.

CAN SCIENCE EXPLAIN RELIGION?

Introduction

A Voice from the Border of Religion and Science

Can science explain religion? "Yes," shouts a strident chorus. Not just explain, but explain away. Gone. Gone for good. "Never" replies an equally adamant crowd. Religion is sacred. It can never be explained by science. In the last few decades, the centuries' old debate between "belief" and "unbelief" has entered new territory. Antireligious polemicists are convinced that the application of the new sciences of the mind to religious belief gives them the final weapons in their battle against irrationality and superstition. A trickle of research papers scattered in specialized scientific journals has now become a torrent of books, articles, and commentary in the popular media; all pressing the case that the cognitive science of religion can finally fulfill the enlightenment dream of eliminating irrationality and superstition and shrinking religion into insignificance, if not eliminating it altogether.

The anthropologist Jesse Bering is reported to have said that now "We've got God by the throat and I'm not going to stop until one of us is dead. . . . It [cognitive science] is going to dry up even the most verdant suburban landscapes and leave spiritual leaders with their tongues out, dying for a drop of faith." The philosopher Daniel Dennett, in a book entitled *Breaking the Spell*—the spell that religion casts over culture—writes that science shows that religion's "mists of incomprehension and failure of communication are not just annoying impediments to rigorous refutation; they are themselves design features of religion." And the point of biologist Richard Dawkins's book *The God Delusion* is clear from the title.

This debate has moved out of the scholarly journals and academic conferences and into the public domain. Militantly anti-religious polemics, supposedly based in cognitive science, have graced the bestseller lists and appeared on television specials. It is this discussion in the popular media that I am addressing in this book. This is not a book for specialists. It is for the general reader and the student new to these topics.

How strong are these claims that cognitive science can explain, or explain away, religion? How compelling are the arguments and the evidence behind them? And if they fall short of their promise, are there still important things to be learned? Answering those questions is the task of this book.

This book thus sits on the boundary between science and religion, a boundary I have lived with and worked on for over forty years. I started teaching religion and science in the militantly secular milieu of a public university in 1971. While students were intrigued, faculty colleagues from a variety of disciplines were appalled; appalled at the idea of putting science and religion together in the same room, on the same course outline. The course almost didn't get approved by the faculty. And that's how the work has gone ever since: a lot of interest, a lot of contention. And teaching in a department of religious studies means that I approach these concerns from a comparative, world-religions perspective and not from the viewpoint of any particular tradition alone.

Besides a PhD in philosophy of religion, I have a second doctorate in clinical psychology and licenses to practice in

New Jersey and New York. And for over thirty years I have practiced as a psychologist. My training involved not only cognitive psychology—I did my thesis on cognition and emotion in depression—but also neuropsychology. And my practice includes what is now popularly called "mind-body medicine" or psychophysiology, biofeedback, and hypnosis. So my thinking about cognitive science takes place against a background of applied clinical work.

The practice of religion, as well as the study of it, is also a part of my life. I am an active priest in the Episcopal Church. I have carried on a long-time, if rather intermittent, meditative discipline in both the Christian and Buddhist traditions. My wife, Kathleen, and I have conducted retreats on contemplative practices both Eastern and Western. We go fairly regularly on retreat ourselves. I have also trained in martial arts at a fairly high level. I am also an associate of an Anglican Benedictine monastic community. While I am not there on retreat as often as I wish, the monastic spirituality built around worship, chanting, meditation, and work buttresses my conviction that religion and science, too, are sets of practices more than systems of belief, and that understanding requires doing. This conviction that religion is a practice first and a set of beliefs second forms part of the background of this book.

So it is from a plurality of perspectives that I come to this investigation of the uses of cognitive science to study, understand, and perhaps undermine religion: the philosopher's concern for reflective and critical analysis; the scientist's concern for rigorous and disciplined investigation; the clinician's concern for human suffering and the vicissitudes of human experience; and the spiritual practitioner's concern for personal transformation and the love of wisdom. While I tend to keep these various facets of my life as separate and compartmentalized as possible, still the academic community and the classroom, the clinic and its professional associations, the church and the meditation hall, as well as Kathleen and our family, all form a network of communities of responsibility that I am accountable to. Do they always see things the same way? Certainly not! Do they sometimes pull me in opposite directions? Certainly! But I am accountable in what I say and write, to be as responsive as possible to their particular concerns. In the cognitive science and religion discussion, any claim to objectivity is illusory. Everyone who discusses this topic has an acknowledged or unacknowledged interest in it, whether one is using cognitive science to undermine religion, defend religion, or simply understand it better. No one can legitimately wrap themselves in the mantle of science and feign objectivity. No one can legitimately come down from the mount of religious experience and proclaim that they see through the eyes of God. For me too, in different ways, these multiple perspectives all enter into the writing of this book.

Chapter 1 provides an overview of the major claims of this new cognitive science of religion. The cognitive science approach to religion concentrates on specific beliefs which are said, by its proponents, to be foundational in all living religions: beliefs in supernatural agents and beliefs in life after death. There is also work being done on religious rituals, but that will not be a central focus here. Rather, this book will follow the current mainline of investigation in the cognitive science of religion and deal primarily with its accounts of the particular religious beliefs on which it focuses: belief in supernatural agents and in life after death.

The core of religion, on these terms, is thus belief in things that go beyond our ordinary, physical world: transcendental powers and life beyond the grave. Whether such beliefs are really central to all that we mean by religion is a contested issue. I once taught a course the goal which was to come up with a definition of religion. After spending sixteen weeks surveying that terrain, the class concluded that no one definition could cover everything that could be labeled "religion." But since this is a book on a particular approach to religion, contemporary cognitive science, we will take it on its own terms and limit ourselves to describing and analyzing their theories regarding beliefs in realities beyond the physical world, such as gods, spirits, ancestors, angels, ghosts, and souls. Many writers today argue that cognitive science explains those beliefs. We will explore the strengths and weaknesses of the explanations they offer, and we will find both. But we will not leave it there. We also will address a deeper issue that is implicit here: Given the theories of cognitive science about such beliefs, how compelling can these beliefs be? Conversely, how compelling is the rejection of these beliefs?

Two important, and I think accurate, claims about religion follow from these investigations: First, that all religious thinking and experiencing is mediated through our cognitive and neurological systems. That is simply a way of saying that religion, as people practice it, is a human phenomenon that can be investigated with the same psychological and neurological tools used to study any human phenomenon. Second, since they are neurologically and cognitively mediated, religious beliefs are limited by the same constraints that affect all domains of human understanding. Cognitive science lays out some of those constraints.

There is a certain personal irony in my writing this book. In the 1980s, when I first began writing about, analyzing, and studying religion using clinical, psychological models, I vociferously argued for exactly those same claims, that religion is a human phenomenon involving natural, psychological processes. Thus I regularly encountered the same charge of "reductionism" in the study of religion. These same issues now recur in the cognitive science of religion. So let me be as clear as I can at the outset: I strongly insist on the necessity and legitimacy of studying religion scientifically and psychologically. And the cognitive science of religion is often a valuable and insightful addition to the ongoing scientific investigation of religion. While I will argue vigorously in the coming pages against some of the interpretations placed on some of the current findings of that project, nothing I say should be interpreted as denying the legitimacy of the project itself. But I am often forcefully struck that exactly the same concerns, voiced thirty years ago, about the psychoanalytic study of religion, are now repeated in relation to the cognitive science of religion, and struck too about how little awareness there seems to be in both the religious and the cognitive science communities about how these issues were previously addressed and resolved. I will return to that observation at various points in the coming pages.

Cognitive science aims to describe some of the ways our minds function in organizing, combining, and remembering information, in this case information related to religion in the broadest sense. Such studies describe processes implicated in believing something religious, but I will suggest that they do not pretend to explain the nature and origin of those beliefs. To do that, the findings of cognitive science must be combined with evolutionary models. Evolutionary models provide the necessary explanatory resources. This marriage of cognitive science and evolutionary models claims for itself the ability to address the origin and nature of religious belief. All this will be briefly described in the first chapter.

At the moment I am composing this, I would say that, based on their writings, three different groups in western Europe and North America are using cognitive studies of religion in three radically different ways by. The first group I call "the debunkers." They are explicitly on a crusade to use cognitive science as a means to undermine and possibly do away with religion once and for all. This is probably the largest group writing for the general public about cognitive and neural science approaches to religion. Their claims seem to predominate in the popular media. In this group I would include Daniel Dennett, Richard Dawkins, Paul Bloom, Pascal Boyer, and Jesse Bering. They are the focus of this book.

The second group I call "the scientists." There are good scientists in all three groups; but the goal of this group is not primarily to debunk, as it is for the first group, or support religion, as it is for the next group. Their goal is mainly to use cognitive science to simply understand religion better. Some in this group may be rather antireligious and some more open to religion. The point is not personalities but rather the primary function of their scientific discussion. In this group I would put Scott Atran, Patrick McNamara, Wesley Wildman, and my colleague Fraser Watts. Their research underlies much of what I say here; they are not the objects of my argument.

The third group I call "the apologists." They want to claim that the findings of cognitive science are explicitly compatible with a particular religious outlook. Here I would place Justin Barrett, a committed Christian; Francis Varela, a long-time Buddhist practitioner; and maybe Andrew Newburg and the late Gene D'Aquile, who appear to me to be arguing that their neuroimaging research is supportive of the truth of certain types of religious experience.

I have no particular stake in this typology. My point is not where individuals might be located on it. I may well have gotten that wrong. My point is rather that cognitive science research, strictly speaking, is religiously neutral. It can be deployed in many different ways in relation to the actual belief in and practice of religion: to undermine it, to simply study it, to support it. These are differences in the interpretation of the data from the cognitive science of religion. I will be arguing that these differences in interpretation at an explicit, reasoned level are driven in part by tacit intuitions and sensibilities at an implicit level. I will draw on the findings from cognitive science to explain how that works. In this book I am concerned with the first group, the antireligious debunkers. Their interpretations and explanations will be the focus of the coming pages.

Before we analyze their claim to having explained religion, we need to understand something about what such a claim might mean. Having surveyed in chapter 1 some of the theories about religion offered by contemporary cognitive science, chapter 2 looks more deeply into the question of what it might mean to explain religion in this way. The second chapter describes in some detail three characteristics of all explanations, scientific or otherwise: (1) explanations are constructed against a "background" of assumptions and viewpoints which, I will argue, often depend on more "intuitive or tacit" cognitions; (2) explanations are always selective in what they attend to; and (3) explanations perform specific functions. Together, these three characteristics imply, I will argue, that all explanations are necessarily incomplete in a variety of senses. This claim of the inevitable incompleteness(es) of all explanatory systems will play an important role in the exploration of cognitive science and religion that follows.

Of particular importance for the coming discussion is the first point, about explanations depending on "tacit" or "intuitive" assumptions. This will be spelled out in more detail in chapter 2. Briefly, my model here is that all investigations operate on at least three levels: (1) there is an overt or explicit, publicly accessible level: the laboratory techniques used in a physical science, the diagnostic practices of medicine, the canons of historical scholarship in history, the rituals, meditative disciplines, and interpretative practices of a religion; (2) these overt practices and procedures depend on background assumptions and beliefs that often result from judgments we make about what appears to us to be true to our experience of the world and useful for making sense of that experience; and (3) these judgments about what assumptions we consider correct are, in turn, influenced by a more tacit or intuitive level involving our basic sensibilities about the world and human nature, including the possible existence or nonexistence of any conceivable transcendental powers or realities.

For example, a patient comes to me with a serious gastrointestinal pain, for which his physician can find no apparent physical cause. I take a detailed history, an explicit practice. I am particularly looking for stressful situations in his life because I assume there is a connection between stress and gastrointestinal distress, an assumption that I have judged to be correct in many cases, based on research findings and clinical experience. This assumption makes sense to me because of my basic intuition that human distress has causes that can be discovered. Any overt diagnostic activity I undertake assumes that there are particular, often psychological processes that play a role in human distress. That assumption reflects, in turn, my more basic belief that causes, including psychological causes, operate in the world. The nature of those causes may be very complex and poorly understood. And there may be more processes at work in the world than those purely causal ones. Nevertheless, I am committed to the belief that such causes are there and can be understood sufficiently well to diagnose a patient's distress and design a helpful intervention. If I were deeply convinced that the world was purely random I would not look for causes or engage in any diagnostic procedures; on that basis my assumption that there are causes to be found would not make sense. Likewise, if I were deeply convinced that the picture of the physical world found in current natural science described, at least potentially, all that is real, I would never consider undertaking a spiritual practice or investigating the claims made by a religious tradition. On the other hand, if I had an intuition that there might be more to reality than what is scientifically describable, I might be open to a further consideration of religious claims.

Support for this three-tiered model (overt practices based on background assumptions grounded in fundamental intuitions about the world) from logic and from cognitive science, as well as the relationships between these three levels, are elaborated in chapter 2. I suggest that disputes between science and religion often involve not scientific data itself, but rather background assumptions and the more basic convictions on which these assumptions rest. This claim is then applied to the explanations of religion supplied by cognitive science and some of the disputes surrounding them.

While there are several different ways of interpreting and using the findings of the cognitive science of religion, the second chapter singles out for attention the antireligious crusaders who seek to use cognitive science to debunk and undermine religion. Their discussion of religion is addressed in some detail in this second chapter with particular attention to the background assumptions that drive their interpretation of the cognitive science of religion and that make it compelling to them. I suggest that part of that background is their judgment that the physical world is the only existing reality and that, therefore, natural science is the only valid path to knowledge. For shorthand purposes, I label that rather narrow viewpoint "physicalism." Its clearest expression is the oft-quoted statement by the American philosopher Wilfrid Sellers, "science is the measure of all things, of what is that it is, and of what is not that it is not." Thus "physicalism," as I use it here, is inevitably reductionist. That is the context in which the arguments of the debunkers of religion and their interpretations of the findings of cognitive science make sense. Whether one thinks those findings, so far, debunk religion or simply help us understand it better primarily depends on whether or not one finds a narrow and reductive physicalism intuitively compelling. Later, I also discuss the additional possibility of nonreductive forms of physicalism.

At a tacit level, I suspect that such antireligious crusaders intuitively feel that physicalism is correct and compelling. But is it really so compelling? These debunkers of religion seem to think that physicalism is synonymous with science. Is that really true? Chapter 3 takes up those questions. The chapter moves directly into a confrontation, not with cognitive science, but with those who think the findings of cognitive science undermine religion and make its beliefs less compelling. I suggest that their debunking assertions about religion go far beyond the actual scientific data in cognitive science, and that move is reasonable only in a purely physicalist framework. Several reasons are offered as to why a purely physicalist framework may not be so compelling and is not synonymous with science. The chapter also discusses the possible limits on evolutionary theory in providing additional explanatory power in relation to religion and other cultural institutions.

Chapter 4 goes even further. Drawing on my clinical work in behavioral medicine, it argues that even revised forms of physicalism are unable to account for the findings arising from that clinical practice. Part of that argument concerns the requirement that, if cognitive science is going to explain religion in a strong sense, there be very tight, direct linkages between neural firings, unconscious cognitive mechanisms, and our religious beliefs. That requirement would not be met if the causal connections among these levels were more complex and reciprocal. Behavioral medicine implies that is the case. In addition, it demonstrates further the inadequacies of the physicalist model on which cognitive science's debunking of religion depends. If physicalism and its very wide-ranging evolutionary models are not as compelling or intuitively obvious as the debunkers of religion hope, where does that leave the enterprise of explaining, and in some cases explaining away, religion by the use of cognitive science? One answer is in expanding our models of nature beyond a narrow physicalism, an option sketched here.

While the first four chapters carry through the idea of debunking the debunkers, the fifth chapter goes beyond undermining the arguments of those who seek to undermine religion. It develops constructive and positive ways to relate science and religion by building on the suggestion that disagreements about the uses of cognitive science occur between those who interpret cognitive science in a purely physicalist context and those who are less devoted only to physicalism. Disagreements at that more tacit and intuitive level cannot be resolved by compelling proofs or coercive demonstrations, since any proofs or demonstrations depend on the very assumptions and viewpoints that are in dispute. But discussion can still take place and reasons for each position can be given. However, the reasons given will most likely be pragmatic. Some pragmatic reasons are then listed that might support a viewpoint that rejects physicalism and affirms a reality beyond the world as described by contemporary natural science. This is not a zero-sum game. If we accept that all explanations are limited and incomplete, we can live happily in a pluralistic universe. While this book is limited to cognitive science, it outlines some implications for the general relationship between science and religion.

It should be clear by now that "religion" is treated at a very general level in this book and in cognitive science. There is no attempt to analyze, critique, or support any particular religious tradition. The goal of this book is not to defend either a general religious outlook or a particular religious tradition, but only to suggest that while there is much to learn from the cognitive scientific study of religion, attempts to use it to "explain" or debunk religion are exaggerated and misguided. That interpretative exaggeration is often driven by the conviction, here called "physicalism," that all that is really real is confined to the physical world as understood, potentially or actually, by current natural science. Conflicts over the interpretation of cognitive science may well be conflicts over the truth of that basic conviction. In that sense this is a book about physicalism and its discontents.

In their paper on the "question of physicalism," Tim Crane and D. H. Mellor conclude that theirs "should really be the last paper on the subject." But they "fear it will not be." My hope is that this book will be the last one on the subject of whether cognitive science weakens or undermines religious commitment. But I too fear that it will not be.

Chapter 1

Explanations

How Science Seeks to Explain Religion

Today, most scientists rely primarily on cognitive psychology and neuroscience in their quest to understand religious beliefs and practices. The assumption here is that religious beliefs and experiences, regardless of tradition, can be accounted for by the same cognitive structures and processes involved in all other aspects of human life. Religion does not require any unique psychological or neurological capacities that are specifically "religious." Another assertion is that differences among religions occur within more general and basic cognitive constraints; any differences between religions are variations of the same cognitive processes underlying all religious beliefs and practices. As I once heard a cognitive scientist studying religion exclaim, "there is only one religion; there are minor variations at the periphery."

Basic Concepts: Schema

Several fundamental concepts are employed by cognitive scientists seeking to understand religion. They are drawn from the general field of cognitive psychology and apply to all domains of human experience. They are not in any way unique to religion or to the cognitive science of religion (CSR). These constructs are shared by virtually all cognitive scientists, not just the "debunkers," who are the focus of this book.

One such claim is that the mind employs "cognitive schema" to process information. Schemas organize and structure our experience. We have schemas that govern what it means to be a "person," that organize our sense of our "self," for domains like "friendship" or "moral responsibility," and especially if religion is important to us either as a practitioner or a debunker, for "god" or "religion" or "spirituality." Different schemas not only organize different content, but also vary in how important they are to us and how much content they contain. My schema for football is rather simple (I don't know much about it) and is rather distant (I don't care that much). My schema for psychopathology is, I hope, more complex and more immediately accessible. I rely on it regularly in my work.

Scientists find that more frequently used schemas process relevant information more quickly than information not associated with any existing schema. The mind also tries to fit any new information into already-existing schemas. This is more efficient, but can create problems for understanding if the new information is not readily assimilated into the old schema. Aspects of the new information that are not congruent with the existing schema may be neglected or ignored. The more efficient processing of schema-relevant information makes laboratory studies of cognitive processing possible. If information is responded to quickly, that suggests that the subject has a well-developed schema for that topic. If the response comes more slowly, that suggests the subject has not developed a readily accessible schema for it. Or if, for example, a person is quickly shown a deck of cards where the cards with hearts are actually black and the cards with spades are red, they will "see" the hearts as red and the spades as black since that is what their card-color schema expects.

Extensive research demonstrates that schemas function to highlight some aspects of an experience and to downplay or hide others. If I have a well-developed schema that attends to human motivation and I go to an opera with someone who is an expert in musicology, I may well miss the subtleties of musical composition and performance. I do not notice a subtle progression of chords in the opening introduction, or that the concluding duet begins and ends in a different key, or that timbre of the tenor's voice does not really match the "color" of the piece he is singing. I have no schema for these things. On the other hand my musicologist colleague overlooks the way in which love in the first act sets up a turn to hate and revenge in the opera's finale. Both dimensions, and many more, are there in the opera, but our separate schemas allow us to easily pick out one set of dimensions and, in turn, conceal the others from us. This will become important when we discuss the process of explanation in the next chapter.

Cognitive schemas, while often unconscious, are usually understood in cognitive science to be the result of learning. Evolutionary cognitive science, as we shall see, also proposes that there are more basic forms of understanding that simply come naturally to human beings and that do not have to be learned in any conscious way. These are often called "folk beliefs," as in "folk physics" or "folk psychology." They appear to come easily and naturally to human minds and are almost always contrasted with the beliefs that are the result of effortful scientific work. That these basic beliefs appear to arise so naturally suggests to the evolutionary cognitive psychologist that they are the result of our evolutionary history and so are subject to selection pressures that bias them toward survival and reproductive fitness. These evolved, natural cognitions play a central role in the evolutionary CSR and its deployment by those who seek to undermine religious convictions.

Basic Concepts: Cognitive Subsystems

Another cognitive-science finding relevant to religion that will be very important to the discussion in the coming chapters is that the human mind contains at least two systems for processing information. These can also be thought of as two levels of cognition. The first is ordinarily unconscious; its contents and its operations are often outside our awareness. This semiunconscious dimension is expressed by calling this system "tacit" or "intuitive." Fraser Watts calls it the "implicational" subsystem. It contains the material we take for granted or consider "obvious" or "self-evident." It produces results that are quick and automatic. It yields what we often call "snap judgments" and "first impressions." Little or no concentration or energy is required here. The second system or level is conscious and is usually referred to as being "reflective." It is slower, deliberate, involves mental effort and is relatively less emotional. This system produces reasoned arguments and thoughtful analysis. Fraser Watts refers to it as a "propositional" subsystem.

We must not forget that these two systems often work together. For example, the immediate results from the tacit, intuitive system often generate the basic assumptions on which the reflective system works. Our intuitive sense that events have causes drives us to look for causes when we confront a perplexing situation. If the lights go out in our house, we check the circuit breaker box. If everything is fine there, we call the power company. Our problem-solving reasoning is guided by our intuition that there must be a cause somewhere. In that sense the intuitive system is often the foundation for what goes on at the conscious, rational level. This finding from cognitive psychology will be a very important part of the discussion that follows in this book, particularly when we discuss the nature of explanation. So most often the intuitive system governs our rational thinking unless the more reflective system puts forth a great deal of effort to analyze and override the activity of the intuitive system. We will shortly see that much cognitive science research suggests that we intuitively see the world in ways that naturally give rise to belief in god or gods. Religious leaders build upon and elaborate upon these intuitions; skeptics call on us to put effort into using our conscious reason to override these intuitions. But, of course, that skeptical use of reason is also guided by intuitive assumptions about how the world works. They are simply different from those that drive the reasoning of the religious.

Although it is sometimes assumed that the intuitive process-ing system is primarily for emotional material while the reflec-tive system is for more detached and intellectual material, it is important to remember that is not necessarily true. The intui-tive system contains concepts and not just feelings, and ideas processed by the reflective system often have affects associ-ated with them. Emotional material is not always processed intuitively, nor is intellectual material necessarily processed reflectively. Both propositional and affective material can be pro-cessed deliberately and reflectively or quickly and immediately. We might find we have an immediate and automatic dislike for some ideas and an immediate positive response to others. Ideas can appear abstract to one person and be passionately evocative for another. Debates about theological topics between antireli-gious skeptics and committed believers often have this flavor. The same religious concepts may be experienced as obtuse and virtually meaningless to the skeptic and life-transforming to the believer. From a cognitive-science standpoint, this is because the skeptic is processing the religious ideas only in an abstract or detached mode, while the religious devotee is processing them in a way that brings more color and vividness to them. Abstract ideas can often provoke highly emotional responses, as anyone who has listened to debates between antagonistic philosophers or theologians can testify to. Again, from this perspective, these intellectual ideas have become closely linked to affective systems. And all current researchers agree that emotion impacts cognition. When we are sad or depressed, we remember negative events more than positive ones and our minds seem to work more slowly. When we are afraid, we are more apt to see the world in black-and-white terms.

An important claim here is that much of what governs our thinking and experiencing is unconscious and out of our awareness and control. We may not be aware of how much our conscious reasoning is governed by assumptions and sensibilities that are outside our conscious awareness. The way we see the world just seems obvious and self-evident to us. Nor do we experience the functioning of the schemas that organize our experience. We do not experience a familiar card-color schema operating to fashion our experience. We just see the cards with hearts on them as red, even if they are actually black. We are not aware of the operation of these varied physiological processes. We just find that we think more negatively when we are sad. Nor are we aware that we respond to some material, for which we have schemas, more quickly than others. The differences in reaction times are too small to enter awareness. Laboratory equipment is necessary to record it.

Basic Concepts: Modularity

Another important assumption in much current cognitive science, and especially the cognitive science that seeks to explain religion, is that the mind is structured as a series of modules. This modular model of the mind is closely associated with the field of Artificial Intelligence and the project of constructing a computer that could represent the world and process information. This paradigm of the mind as a series of rather independent modules designed to represent the world and process information is often referred to as the "Cognitivist paradigm." Here the mind is not understood as a general, all-purpose information-gathering system but rather as a series of discrete modules—how discrete and separate is a matter of great controversy—each specialized for a specific task. Thus there are "perceptual modules" for processing visual, tactile, auditory information, such as a facial-recognition module or a color-discrimination module. There are also emotional-processing modules that organize our experiences of anger, joy, sadness, etc. And there are more purely conceptual modules that structure our thinking along certain pathways. These modules are understood to operate more or less unconsciously, automatically, and independently to produce the experiences, beliefs, and activities that constitute our lives. Processes like agency detection or thinking that other people have thoughts and feelings are seen by many cognitive psychologists as central to religion. They are understood as the automatic result of the operation of such underlying cognitive modules.

As just noted, the question of how discrete and separate are these modules is matter of great ongoing controversy in basic neurology and in cognitive science. For one thing, any modularity at the cognitive level does not map well onto basic neurology. One of the deeply perplexing things about neurology is the complex, sometimes paradoxical, interrelation of both the localization and the holistic systemic functioning found in the brain and the rest of the central nervous system (CNS). Certainly we have localized areas in the brain, like Broca's Area for speech production. If that area is injured, speech suffers. But speech production involves much more than Broca's Area. To produce speech, Broca's Area interacts intensely with other parts of the brain. To become speaking subjects we need those auditory areas involved in hearing and recognizing speech. We need the higher cortex to mediate the thoughts we put into speech. We need the motor areas controlling the movements of lips and tongue. And we engage the whole somatosensory cortex, since we usually turn to face the person we are speaking to and look at them. We speak with our whole brain and body, not just with Broca's Area. Sometimes when one area of the brain is damaged, other areas not "localized" for that function can be trained to take it up. Also when we look at scans of the functioning brain, we see activity all throughout the CNS, not just in a localized "module."

Much current evidence suggests that the living, active brain does not function so much like a series of autonomous or semi-autonomous modules operating in linear sequences, but rather as a reciprocally interacting and mutually influencing system, from which emerges, sometimes in different ways at different times, increasingly complex and interconnected neuronal patterns. For example, studies of particular sensations, smells, vision, etc., show that there is no simple single set of neuronal connections and patterns. The pattern associated with a particular sight, smell, or taste can differ from individual to individual, depending on the animal's history, which formed its particular pattern of synaptic connections. These neurological markings do not "represent" a predator or a poison in some direct, literal way since the patterns are constantly shifting and vary from individual to individual. One author has noted that "physically distinct brain states may generate identical or near-identical *cognitive properties.*" Therefore, theories depending on direct, linear connections between specific modules and particular cognitions involved in very complex processing, may have limited applicability and very weak explanatory power. The neurology of experience, therefore, seems better represented by nonlinear dynamical models than models of lineal causation, where a particular sight or smell is claimed to always produce the exact same neuronal effect. In nonlinear dynamical systems there are continually shifting patterns, in this case of neurons firing, that are also constrained within certain limits. From these continually reciprocating processes, new stimulations continuing to come into the brain, neighboring neurons firing, etc., emerge those sensations we experience as smell, sight, taste, etc. These basic physiological structures and the patterns of neuronal firing they give rise to are shaped and reshaped by the animal's behavioral history, the experiences it encountered along the way and its current activity. Such a nonlinear, complex model is the opposite of the "massive modularity" model that appears to still dominate the theorizing found in CSR.

Much current CSR, especially that dedicated to undermining religion, appears to rely heavily on the two assumptions that define the Cognitivist standpoint: that the mind is a computer, an information-processing machine designed to answer practical questions by using rule-governed programs whose symbols mirror objective aspects of the world; and that the mind is made up of individual, discrete cognitive modules "designed" into our hunter-gatherer forebears by natural selection because they successfully furthered survival and reproduction. As we have stressed, the modularity assumption is highly contested and does not map well onto current neurophysiological findings, which emphasize wholism, integration, and emergence, and probably nonlinear dynamics, as well as reciprocal interactions with the environment. Nor is the mind/brain simply the passive recipient of sensory "input" that represents the world, but rather it actively creates and constructs its experience of the world. The idea of the mind as a passive "mirror" of nature (Rorty) is hard to defend after decades of research in cognitive psychology. Such a claim is often simply asserted, not demonstrated. It is not clear what would even count as a demonstration.

Concerns like this have caused much cognitive science to retreat from the radical modularity hypothesis of early 1980s that characterized the early Cognitivist paradigm. In his 2006 book, Peter Carruthers attempts to defend again the massive-modularity hypothesis. Two things seem clear, though, about this book. First, his modules are not as massively modular—that is as self-contained, separate, and specialized—as the earlier theories maintained. Nor are they as modular as is required to support CSR's frequent reliance on a method that simply breaks religion down into isolated and discreet components, analyzes them without reference to each other or any larger internal psychological or external cultural contexts, and then claims to have provided an explanation of religion. Second, having revised and constricted the modularity hypothesis, Carruthers still has probably not addressed the general problems with the modularity hypothesis in a compelling way. To the extent that its theorizing depends on a strong modular model, the theorizing of CSR appears to be in trouble. Justin Barrett appears to have backed away from a strong modularity and instead refers to "mind tools" and "maturationally natural abilities," and now says he is committed to "only a very weak modularity," but he also affirms "that some do adhere to a stronger version." And Robert McCauley, in his book on why religion is natural, also avoids the issue of modularity. It remains to be seen whether this "very weak modularity" is sufficiently strong to support the kinds of methods and arguments found among those who seek to use CSR to debunk religion.

Clearly some cognitive processes are relatively self-contained. For example, we seem to have prepared capacities to develop certain kinds of taste aversions or phobias more rapidly than happens with regular learning. Likewise, with facial-recognition abilities. So we can be said to have specific cognitive substructures for learning those things. But this is relatively rare. So we need to be alert to the extent to which much of the debunking use of the CSR still relies on the more extreme Cognitivist modular models in its theorizing.

A Cognitive Science of Religion

So far we have just reviewed some of the basic concepts from cognitive science that have proven relevant to understanding religion. None of these claims to offer an "explanation" of religion. They describe only some of the cognitive processes hypothetically involved in all human pursuits, including religion. No one claims these general processes caused religion to arise in human history or that they explain why people are religious today. But these psychological models form the context in which cognitive explanations of religion are constructed. There are two important implications of these types of scientific models about religion.

First, they presuppose that all religious thinking and experiencing, like all human thought and experience, is neurologically and cognitively mediated. Every experience, thought, or feeling comes to us through our brains and our cognitive processing systems. This is a necessary working assumption in all cognitive and neuroscience. If some aspect of human existence is going to be studied scientifically, it must show up on brain scans or in laboratory experiments studying how the mind organizes and processes information. These are two types of investigation central to contemporary cognitive neuroscience. The fact that to date, all religious experiences that have been brought into the neurology lab and subject to brain scans have, in fact, shown up on brain scans is very strong, virtually conclusive, evidence that such experiences are neurologically mediated and that this assumption is correct. If there were some aspect of human existence that was not cognitively and neurologically mediated, it could not be studied scientifically. But if it was not mediated in this way, it is hard to know how we could come to experience it, understand it, and encode it in our memory.

This assumption does not entail that every aspect of human existence is purely physical, that is, it does not rule out dualism. It entails only that if there were in reality a nonphysical aspect to human nature we would know about it and experience it only through our neurological and cognitive apparatus. Thus its effects, if not its existence, could be studied scientifically. As a working assumption, it does not even logically rule out the possibility of experiences that are not neurologically mediated. It simply sets a domain limit to scientific investigation: that only those experiences that are neurologically mediated can be studied by science. But any claim that there are experiences not neurologically mediated would require very strong evidence in order to be taken seriously. And if such evidence were offered, that would bring the claim within the domain of science. And if the evidence proved demonstrable and compelling, that would require a major revision, virtually a scientific revolution, in our understanding of human nature. Nothing short of a scientific revolution would be necessary to make such a claim compelling scientifically. And that is a very high bar to reach.

Second, since religion is cognitively and neurologically mediated, it is constrained by the limits and structures of our neural-cognitive nature. And, of course, the same is true of all human activities, including cognitive science itself, as well as art, politics, literature, etc. All human activities take place within certain constraints. As we will see, one of the major projects in CSR is explicating more exactly what those constraints are.

Evolutionary Approaches

So, theories about how the religious mind functions by themselves do not explain where religion comes from or why people believe in it. These theories only claim to "explain" religion when they become joined with evolutionary models which offer an account of how the mind came to function in the way that cognitive scientists find that it does. From the merger of cognitive models, which are mostly derived from laboratory experiments and are not necessarily based on evolutionary theories and evolutionary psychology, which primarily makes claims about how the mind evolved by the Darwinian dynamic of natural selection, the claim to "explain" religion arises.

The core of Darwin's theory was natural selection, often called "the survival of the fittest." But that leaves open the question of the meaning of the "fittest." For most of those who follow Darwin today, the "fittest" means those who have the most offspring. This follows from the combination of Darwin's natural selection with later theories of genetics. The fittest are those who reproduce the most. For Darwin, who did not know about modern genetic theory, the fittest were simply those who survived the vicissitudes of living. For Darwin that usually meant those who were best adapted to their environment and were thus able to survive and thrive within it. This has led to at least three different ways of applying evolutionary theory to religion: (1) to argue that if religion has survived for millennia, which it certainly has, it must be adaptive in some way; (2) to apply Darwinian models to ideas, and in this case religious ideas, and to argue that religious ideas themselves have certain characteristics that make them likely to survive and propagate, just as some lucky people have traits that make them more likely to survive and so propagate more; and (3) to use evolutionary models to explain the origin of the cognitive systems which give rise to religion.

Some scientists argue for the possible adaptive function of religious beliefs and practices. Many social scientists have claimed that religious beliefs and rituals strengthen group cohesion. If a community holds beliefs and engages in rituals that reinforce trust, good will, and cooperation, such a community would be stronger, and so would be safer from predators, and more cooperative, and so more successful in hunting game. Members of such a community would have a competitive advantage over those in weaker, less cohesive communities. Hence, if there is a genotype, the individual's actual genes, associated with religious beliefs and practices, it would be favored by natural selection.

Common beliefs would likely encourage group cohesion. What might rituals, an important aspect of religion, also contribute here? One answer is that participation in religious rituals suggests to others that one is devoted to the group. Thus these rituals function as "costly signals" of commitment. If a ritual demands a great deal of time, energy, and other resources, that would weed out "free-riders" who take advantage of a community's strength without paying the cost of being a good citizen. Religious rituals can also be understood as accurate evidence of commitment that would be hard for a nonmember to fake. Those who participate in the community's rituals can be accepted as trustworthy, committed members, for they have signaled their commitment at some personal cost. Actually I have combined here two different theories: so called "costly signaling" theories, which stress how rituals weed out "free-riders," and "hard-to-fake" signaling theories, which suggest that ritual involvement is an accurate signal of commitment. Both theories are contested, but studies have provided some support for a connection between ritual participation and cooperation, trust, and altruism.

It is important to note that this argument does not claim that religion arose in order to promote group cohesion. Most scientists reject such an understanding of evolution. Current theory says that adaptive traits and cultural practices arose accidentally, as the result of random genetic mutation. As we shall soon see, most cognitive scientists claim that religion arises as the inevitable result of certain basic cognitive processes and not in order to accomplish any goals, such as reproductive fitness or social cohesion. But once a religious idea or practice arises accidentally through the functioning of the cognitive system and independently of any reproductive or social advantage, it may then provide the group with a reproductive advantage. This advantage then enables this group to survive and prosper. For example, David Sloane Wilson proposes that religious systems which arose independently of this function usually produce cohesive groups that do better than less cohesive societies in the competition for resources and progeny. These types of evolutionary account of religion are all examples of what is called in the literature "group selection"; that is, that it is the survival of the group and not just a few genetically well-endowed individuals that we should consider when assessing survival and adaptation. Such theories are highly controversial in biological circles, but hard to avoid when discussing religion.

So religion may have arisen and spread because its social function conferred survival advantages on religious groups. Such an account does not rely much on cognitive factors. Nor do these evolutionary accounts really explain much about the actual content of religious ideas and practices. For that, more specifically cognitive models are necessary.

Supernatural Agents

Ideas that come naturally to children would be easy to pass on to future generations. Since they are the earliest ideas and the primary ideas with which a person begins to think, they become the fundamental, intuitive assumptions that govern later reasoning. Developmental psychologists have long discovered that religious ideas come naturally to children. Even children raised in militantly atheistic homes are found to naturally believe in god. Why is that so?

Many have suggested that children see adults as godlike and god as human-like. Clearly children, and adults, think of god and other supernatural agents in anthropomorphic terms. And research suggests that very young children usually think of all personal agents as all-powerful and all-knowing. Around age five, children begin to discriminate among the abilities possessed by various agents and to outgrow the tendency to generalize the same exaggerated powers to all possible agents. This implies that children take time to learn the limitations of human powers and that religious notions about all-powerful and all-knowing agents are humanity's primal and fundamental, and therefore intuitive, assumptions about minds and agents. Such cognitive assumptions make the idea of an all-knowing, all-powerful god, or gods, immediately intuitive. Thus the idea of such a divine being or beings would be immediately compelling, easy to come up with, and to communicate, remember, and believe in.

These developmental dynamics would facilitate belief in all-knowing, all-powerful supernatural agents. But again, this cognitive-developmental research describes how the mind appears to function and these natural processes may explain why people find the idea of god or gods compelling. But it offers no explanation of how such cognitive processes arose in the first place. This is where evolutionary theory comes in. In particular, Stewart Guthrie's "anthropomorphism theory" claims that a single evolved cognitive process underlies all religious belief and practice—the recognition of supernatural agency. For Guthrie this belief in supernatural agents is the byproduct of a set of cognitive tendencies that arose accidentally in the course of evolution but persisted because they helped our earliest ancestors survive and reproduce. Calling them a byproduct means that these cognitive tendencies were not selected because they give rise to religion, but for rather different purposes that are more closely connected to survival.

Such byproducts of evolution are called "spandrels," an architectural term for a structure's feature that was accidental but can be put to constructive or decorative use. We remodeled the stairs in our apartment and that created an enclosed space under the stairs. Perfect for a closet, which we desperately needed. We did not redo the stairway in order to create a closet but the new enclosed stairway made the closet possible. Likewise, as we shall soon see, certain cognitive processes were selected for by evolution because they helped our hunter-gatherer ancestors survive. But they also provided the cognitive basis for religion. They did not arise in order to generate religious ideas, but once in place, that was their natural result, like our closet being the natural result of enclosing the stairway.

Guthrie argues that humans have evolved a tendency to look for and focus on beings who appear to be intentional agents with minds analogous to human minds. It makes a certain amount of intuitive sense that we would evolve a tendency to attend to, and perhaps overattend to, other humans and other human-like beings, that is agents with minds, in the service of survival and reproduction. Hence, for survival it would be better to "overdetect" agents, even when their existence was possible but not certain, than to ignore their presence. Better to assume the rock ahead is a bear or the sound in the grass is a lion than to assume it is only a rock or the wind and become their supper. Guthrie argues that we evolved a tendency to overdetect the presence of human-like agency around us. Thus we attribute human-like agency to natural forces and events. Religion, then, is the natural, perhaps inevitable, result of this normal cognitive process, which developed through a kind of cognitive natural selection as a means to survival.

Much laboratory research in cognitive science supports the claim that people attribute agency to ambiguous or clearly nonagentic stimuli. As early as the first five months of life, experiments suggest that infants perceive agency in the self-propelled and purposeful-looking movement of colored disks. And not just infants. The most famous example is a film of two triangles and a circle moving in and around a rectangle with a side that opens and closes. Adult viewers unselfconsciously readily describe the movement of the forms in anthropomorphic, agent language. This apparently natural attribution by adults has been demonstrated time and again in the laboratory. The figures do not have to look like humans or animals or fictional agents. Justin Barrett called this cognitive system the Hypersensitive Agency Detection Device, universally abbreviated as HADD in the literature. Like many of the cognitive processes described here, unless we consciously work to override it, the HADD unconsciously and automatically delivers to us an experience of agency in the face of ambiguous stimuli. We hear a noise in the night and immediately think of an intruder. When we go and investigate, we find it is only a branch blown against the window by an unusually strong wind.

Many cognitive scientists who seek to explain religion rely heavily on the idea of a HADD as a major cause for belief in supernatural agents in both children and adults. However, there is controversy in the literature over exactly what characteristics are necessary to evoke a sense of agency. In the original Heider and Simmel film experiment, the movements of the triangles and the circle were presented to the subjects in what the experimenters themselves refer to as "anthropomorphic words" such as the triangle "moves towards the house, opens the door and enters the house, closes the door," or the two triangles "fight" and one "wins." In one of the three experimental conditions the subjects were specifically asked to respond to questions like "what sort of person is the big triangle, the little triangle, the circle? Why did the circle go into the house?" After instructions like this, the suggestion that this experiment finds some purely natural and spontaneous tendency to use anthropomorphic agent language is questionable in the extreme. In addition, researchers agree that the movements of the objects must appear to have no external cause and, some researchers suggest, these movements cannot be purely random but appear goal-directed, such as reaching or avoiding something, and be aimed at an end result. While the objects do not have to be human or animal, the movements of these inanimate objects seem designed to mimic the actions of agents. And, of course, there is an intentional agent behind these interactions, that is the creator of the experiment. So the claim that we naturally and spontaneously see agency virtually everywhere may be an exaggeration. In addition, we normally very quickly reject any "false positive" intimations produced by HADD. If I find no human or animal intruder in the basement after hearing a strange noise, I do not immediately hypothesize an invisible ghost down there. There is no evidence that my Paleolithic ancestors would react differently in an analogous situation. Religious beliefs, on the other hand, continue being affirmed over long periods of time. Clearly, relatively minor or nonpersonal or ambiguous stimuli can evoke attributions of personal agency, especially when one is primed for it; but there is questioning even within the CSR community about how much explanatory power regarding religion that single, hypothesized cognitive process really has.

Guthrie's theory points to a single cognitive structure that explains the origin of belief in the supernatural agents that populate the religions of the world. But explaining religion requires more than explaining the origin of the idea of god, or even explaining why the idea of god or some other supernatural power is compelling. Explaining religion also requires explaining why the idea of god, once it's generated by HADD or some other process, becomes so widespread in human history and culture. Is pointing to universal cognitive mechanisms underlying religion sufficient to account for the virtually universal spread of religion? Perhaps not. But here too evolutionary concepts, when applied to ideas as well as to species, can be used to supply additional explanations.

The Evolution of Religious Ideas

Pascal Boyer proposes that religious concepts, once they arise, survive and propagate efficiently because they fall within what he calls a "cognitive optimum" of being easily described and communicated but also "counterintuitive" enough to be attention-grabbing and readily remembered. Whereas cognitive theories of the origin of religious ideas stress their natural and intuitive nature, cognitive theories of the propagation of those same ideas stress their counterintuitiveness. The problem seems to be that concepts that fit too well with our intuitions are easy to understand and communicate but are not always all that interesting. But concepts that deviate slightly, in one or two ways, from our ordinary experience might enjoy the gain of making intuitive enough sense, but also be more intriguing and attention-grabbing and therefore evoke more interest and reflection. A tree that just stands there is not usually all that interesting. Few would come home and bother to tell their families that they saw a tree on their way to work. A tree that spontaneously takes off and flies to the moon and disappears into space is just

bizarre and unbelievable. A tree that walks and talks is pictur-
able and also attention-grabbing and easily remembered from a
host of books we read to our children. Likewise with a bush that
burns but is not consumed, or a man who can heal the sick by
touching them.

So widespread religious ideas are not totally counterintuitive and completely bizarre or simply intuitive and ordinary,
but rather what Boyer calls "minimally counterintuitive," often
abbreviated MCI. Minimal counterintuitiveness is formally
defined as changing one feature of a basic cognitive category.
Apparently, children soon develop a "folk" (i.e., "unscientific")
category of "person." A person is embodied, active, and has a
mind. A god or spirit is a person who is not embodied. So gods
and spirits are minimally counterintuitive. Thus they enjoy
that "cognitive optimum," an ideal balance of intuitive and
counterintuitive aspects, and so will be remembered easily and
propagate efficiently. This is one of the cognitive constraints on
religious narratives: they must contain enough normal elements
to be believable and one or two elements that violate our normal
schema for how the world works that will make the narratives
compelling and memorable. Research into the claim that minimally counterintuitive ideas are better remembered and passed
on has produced mixed results. Some studies have supported
Boyer's thesis and some have not, which suggests that this factor is, at best, only a partial element in the spread of religion.

Also one might at least wonder whether what strikes a
postenlightenment materialist as counterintuitive would have
struck our evolutionary ancestors that same way. When we
make claims about counterintuitiveness, we may simply be projecting our own sensibilities back onto our forebears. We have
no idea how they experienced the world. Our current distinc-
tions between the natural and the supernatural, the physical
and the spiritual, appear, at least to some extent, to be the result

of the scientific revolution and the resultant naturalistic world-view. It is at least hypothetically possible that previous generations experienced the world without that dichotomous schema, and so their immediate sensibility about the "natural" and the "supernatural" would have been very different. We simply do not have any solid evolutionary evidence about how our Paleolithic ancestors' minds worked. Developing a theory about that based on research with contemporary children and then projecting it back onto our ancestors seems to assume that evolutionary development follows individual development, that is, early humans were like contemporary children. Many researchers find that a dubious assumption, and no evidence is offered for it here. And some of what we do know suggests otherwise. For example, the "cave paintings" are very far from being "childish." In may be that our precursors saw agency everywhere and distinguished the "natural" from the "supernatural" as we do and thus created the MCI supernatural agents that populate the religions of the world in the way CSR describes. But their experience of the world and themselves could have been vastly different from that postulated here. We simply do not know.

In his 2001 book, Boyer addresses some of these problems, as well as the criticism that there is more to religious ideas than only their possible MCI nature. In addition, Boyer argues that religious concepts must be able to generate useful and important inferences and explanations. Boyer calls this their "inferential potential." If a concept can be useful in a wide range of areas of interest to human beings, it is more likely to get adopted. Should my cognitive processes naturally generate the idea of a supernatural agent; and should my culture supply me with more content than just a supernatural agent—as in the idea of a personal god, or gods, or ancestors, or spirits; and should the idea of this agent provide answers to my naturally occurring questions about the origin of the world and right and wrong; and should my intuitive assumptions from childhood about the reality of an all-knowing, all-powerful person make such an idea feel obvious; that would be a lot of reasons to believe in such a supernatural agent.

In addition, some counterintuitive properties have more "inferential potential" than others, Boyer suggests. The story of a tree that spontaneously flies to the moon and disappears is radically counterintuitive, but few important inferences follow from it. Boyer suggests that agents with minds, human or animal, or even vegetative, have greater inferential potential than nonagents. And so counterintuitive claims that either redescribe a nonagent as an agent (such as a mountain that talks) or that transform the ordinary category of agent in interesting ways (an invisible person or one who walks through walls) have powerful possibilities for remembrance and propagation.

Even more important for Boyer are agents possessing what he terms "strategic information," information necessary for survival and reproduction. Possessing strategic information guarantees the inferential potential of a god, spirit, or ancestor and gives that being authority in the existential domains of health, life and death, surviving, and determining right from wrong: not just knowing right from wrong but being able to reward those who do right and punish those who do wrong. Such agents are at the core of most religions. Given their possession of strategic information, their ability to act in the world, and moral power, such agents evoke worship, prayer, celebration, propitiation, and other ritual responses. So traits such as being all-knowing, all-powerful, and invisible are more likely to be found in religiously important beings than, as Justin Barrett often says, failing to exist on Wednesdays, experiencing time backwards, or giving birth to young of a different species. This is another cognitive constraint upon religious narratives.

Intuitive Dualism and other Religious Ideas

So far we have offered a cognitive explanation for the origin and spread of belief in supernatural agents. Belief in supernatural agents seems to be the defining characteristic of religion for most cognitive psychologists. But there is more to religion than only that belief. For example, virtually all religions have beliefs about a life beyond death. Here too, cognitive psychologists have proposed theories and done research on how various cognitive processes cause us to believe that we, or part of us, might survive death. Obviously, this involves, among other things, the cognitive mechanisms that generate our thoughts about the physical and any possible nonphysical dimensions of humanity. Our ideas about these issues govern whether or not we believe in life after death and, if we do, what form it might take. They also influence any thoughts we might have about the possibility of ghosts, ancestral spirits, angels, and other discarnate beings.

Psychologist Paul Bloom argues that our cognitive processes inevitably make us "intuitive dualists." Bloom claims that we have two representational systems that can conflict. One he calls "naïve" or "folk" physics, which represents objects in our ordinary world as solid, bounded physical objects. It begins working in the first few months of life and gradually comes to represent our bodies too as bounded, solid physical objects. The second system he calls "folk" or "naïve" psychology. It represents the world as filled with agents with minds and begins as soon as the child comes to understand that human beings have minds, that is, have thoughts, feelings, intentions. This representation is often called a "theory of mind," not a theory about the mind but a theory that other beings have minds. A great deal of research suggests that between ages three and five, some research claims even earlier, children start to think of others as being "minded," holding beliefs that can be true or false, forming intentions, and having feelings. The research also suggests, what every parent knows, that children appear to overgeneralize, from the parents' perspective, their "theory of mind" to the pet dog and the stuffed teddy bear. This "theory of mind," the idea that human beings have minds, is the core, then, of what cognitive psychologists often call "folk psychology."

These terms like "folk psychology" or "folk physics" have become virtually technical terms in cognitive psychology. They refer to the primal, intuitive, automatic understandings of how the world works that are general across cultures and provided our ancestors reasonable guidance for making their way through their daily world. Much of this theorizing about "folk" beliefs is derived from studies of how children and some adults spontaneously categorize and understand the objects they encounter in their world. "Folk" beliefs are almost always vigorously contrasted with scientific knowledge, which is seen as rational, objective, verifiable, and gained only through a great deal of effort.

Bloom argues that these two systems, folk physics and folk psychology, develop in children at different ages. They have, he claims, separate evolutionary histories, and process different types of information. Thus they are only loosely connected. They may even conflict, especially when considering humans' self-experience. This loose, even conflictual, relationship between these two representational systems, the physical and the psychological, gives rise to an intuitive, dualistic theory of human nature; or at least makes such a theory compelling when it is encountered. For Bloom, some kind of afterlife belief is a natural extension of folk psychology and intuitive dualism.

Given this intuitive dualism, the idea that something of a person persists after death is very common. In addition, Jesse Bering points to the apparent impossibility of imagining that one no longer possesses consciousness. When combined with

our "intuitive dualism," it is natural to think that consciousness can persist after death. There is also, Bering adds, a natural
human desire not to let go of a loved one who has died, and so
to find meaning in subtle events after the death of a loved one,
such as surprising sights or sounds or dreams, is understand-
able. Such events are easily construed as evidence of the persis-
tence of the other after death. Research suggests that children,
even in atheistic families, naturally develop strong beliefs in an
afterlife.

Bering further claims that having such afterlife beliefs was
selected for in the course of evolution because such beliefs promote prosocial behavior. People who believe that gods, ghosts,
or ancestor spirits are watching them are probably more inclined
to behave in ways that promote social cohesion. Such behavior
is also good for their social standing and so makes them more
attractive sexual partners. Bering calls this a "supernatural
punishment theory" which emphasizes how ideas of constantly
observing, morally concerned, and potentially punishing gods
or spirits would make people more focused on their reputations.
They would be less likely to cheat others, even in secret, because
the gods would know and punish them, even if no human could.
Thus they would become more trusted members of the community, have better success at mating, and enjoy other social
benefits.

Deborah Kelemen and her colleagues have demonstrated
that children engage in what she calls, in a wonderful phrase,
"promiscuous teleology." They see design and purpose in the
natural world beyond what adults normally see. Children tend
to say that rocks are "pointy" because being pointy keeps them
from being sat upon and crushed. They naturally express such
teleological concepts to explain the origin of living things, like
plants and animals, and natural things, like rocks and rivers.
And not just children. Researchers find that adults who lack

much formal education also naturally use teleological explanations to understand nature. Most strikingly, even scientifically
educated adults, when under time pressure to answer questions,
revert to teleological explanations. All this implies that "promiscuous teleology" cannot be simply outgrown developmentally,
but is at best constrained only in highly educated contexts. Even
children from families and schools that insist on evolutionary
accounts of the origin of the species often do not begin accepting
them until after age ten. Such widespread teleological thinking
is a central aspect of "folk physics." Such teleological reasoning
naturally gives rise to, or at least reinforces, the idea that the
world was created for a purpose by an intentional creator. Developmental research consistently finds that children the world
over insist that while people make cars and tables, god makes
trees and mountains.

Summary

So religion is caused by the natural operation of cognitive
mechanisms that were selected by evolution for safety, survival, and ease of transmission, and not for the production of
religious beliefs and practices or to aid in a spiritual search.
Rather, our agency-detection and causation-attribution systems are biased toward safety and survival, so that we avoid
dangerous predators and select appropriate mates. Better to
"detect" agency even where it doesn't exist than to mistake
that bear for a rock. Our predilections to believe in supernatural agents result from the necessary overactivity of such
cognitive systems. Our belief in supernatural agents is the
byproduct of cognitive mechanisms that evolved for reasons of survival unrelated to supernatural beings or spiritual
concerns. We are also inclined to remember narratives that

contain minimally counterintuitive features, that is, narratives that are basically realistic but violate our "folk" categorizations in only one or two ways: superheroes who are human but superstrong or capable of flight, or religious personages who walk on water or possess transcendental insight into the nature of reality and the destiny of the human spirit. Religious narratives are a potent, perhaps the most potent, source of such minimally counterintuitive concepts and images. Religions also build upon our "intuitive" or "folk" beliefs about minds, about there being both physical and nonphysical aspects to human nature, that is, "intuitive dualism," and the naturalness of teleological explanations. After it arises out of the operation of these cognitive mechanisms, which evolved for other reasons, religion can then acquire social functions that do contribute to human survival and reproductive success, and so it becomes adaptive and a staple feature of human history. We are not aware of these cognitive mechanisms, operating outside of our consciousness. Effortful scientific investigation is necessary to uncover them and to counteract our "folk psychology" and to reveal the "real causes" behind religious convictions and practices.

Chapter 2

Explaining

What Does It Mean to Explain Religion?

In the first chapter we reviewed some of the explanations of religion offered by contemporary cognitive science. Then the questions are: What might such explanations mean? And how are they to be understood and interpreted? To answer those questions, we first have to understand something about the nature of explanation itself. When we say something is explained, what sort of claim is that?

The Nature of Explanations

Questions about the nature of scientific explanation, and explanation in general, have been often discussed and highly contested since the start of the scientific revolution. This controversy has centered on questions like: *Is scientific explanation completely rule-governed? Can it be completely described by a formal series of stages or operations?* This is the kind of approach that is often taken in elementary scientific textbooks that begin by laying out a set of steps called the "scientific method." Another question involves whether there is a single type of "scientific explanation," or can different sciences employ different methods yielding different types of explanation but all of them still be considered "scientific" in some sense? Those are not the kinds of questions that I want to discuss in this chapter. I am happy to stipulate that the laboratory research conducted by cognitive scientists is "scientific" in the ordinary sense of that term. I see no reason to dispute that. The question I want to discuss is, given that the findings of cognitive science are "scientific" in some legitimate sense of that term, what does that tell us about these conclusions and explanations?

Three properties or characteristics of all scientific explanations, and of all explanations, are relevant for making sense of and interpreting the findings of the cognitive science of religion: (1) explanations are contextual and constructed against a "background" of assumptions and viewpoints which are judged to be true but are often influenced by our "intuitive" or "tacit" cognitions; (2) explanations are selective; (3) specific explanations perform specific functions.

First, all explanations and the reasons for them are contextual. They take place in a context. They are constructed against what some call a "background." I might claim to explain the nature of the substance we call "water" by saying that it is made up of the elements of hydrogen and oxygen with a ratio of two parts hydrogen to one part oxygen (hence H_2O). I can demonstrate this by applying a low-voltage electric current to a sample of water and thus break it down into two components easily identified as hydrogen and oxygen. But constructing and understanding this elementary chemical experiment requires knowledge of molecular chemistry: what chemical elements are, how they bond together, the role of energy in making and breaking chemical bonds, and many other things as well. These concepts form part of the necessary background to understanding the explanation of even the simplest experiment from the first semester of high school chemistry. Without them, the experiment and the claim that a glass of water contains two invisible components would be literally meaningless.

Or, to take another example from high school, using Euclidian geometry, I can write out a "proof" that describes the necessary structure of a "right triangle," one with a 90° angle. The proof is called the Pythagorean Theorem after the Greek mathematician who worked it out. If I walked into a classroom and saw the steps in the proof written on the blackboard, and if I remembered my high school geometry, I would recognize the proof and understand the steps. But if I had no knowledge of Euclidean geometry, the mathematical symbols would be gibberish and their order would appear totally random. Mathematical proofs too require a context or background in order to be explained and for that explanation to be understood. In this case that background is the axioms of Euclidean geometry and an elementary understanding of formal reasoning.

In order to understand an explanation and find it convincing, I must share the same background. Or, an explanation is only as convincing as is the background within which it is constructed. If, for some reason, I did not share a background in molecular chemistry, the hydrolysis experiment would not convince me that water is really H_2O. If, for some reason, I was skeptical about Euclidean geometry, going over the steps of the Pythagorean Theorem would not prove anything to me. So every explanation and every proof for that explanation requires a context and background assumptions. To fully understand the explanations of religion proffered by cognitive science, we must understand the background against which they are developed. And to find them compelling, we must share that background. This is true of all scientific work.

Notice that while I explain, demonstrate, or prove the correctness of an explanation in the context of a field or discipline, I do not prove the whole discipline correct or true. In the context of Euclidean geometry I can prove the truth of the Pythagorean Theorem, but I do not prove Euclidean geometry true. In the context of molecular chemistry I can demonstrate that water is composed of hydrogen and oxygen, but I cannot demonstrate the truth of the whole field of chemistry. In this sense, every relatively complex field in which reasoning takes place or proofs are constructed is "incomplete," meaning, among other things, that the axioms and assumptions on which it depends cannot themselves be demonstrated within that field. Such a demonstration would in turn require another set of axioms, which, in turn, would be undemonstrated. Demonstrating the truth of a whole field would require locating that field in an even larger field with its own additional, undemonstrated axioms and assumptions. So while I cannot prove the axioms of Euclidean geometry within Euclidean geometry, I can construct models of Euclidean space from which these axioms could be derived. But these models would have their own domains of incompleteness.

This reveals something fundamental about the process of explaining and proving that is illustrated clearly by Euclidean geometry. What we prove depends on what we cannot prove. If I say that I will not accept anything without evidence, proof, or warrant, I am immediately caught in an infinite regress of evidence for evidence, proofs for proofs, warrants for warrants. Obviously I do not employ an infinite regress of proofs following other proofs every time I make a claim. At some place I stop that potentially infinite regress. And I stop it at some place that I do not prove; rather I make a judgment that I will accept those assumptions or axioms and commit myself to them. I hope I make a reasoned judgment about what to accept as a starting point. But it is a judgment, not a proof.

The proofs of Euclidean geometry depend on accepting the axioms of Euclidean geometry. Without accepting these axioms, no proofs could be constructed. We might even go so far as to say, since this is a book about science and religion, that where we stop is a point that we do not prove but that we take on faith in the sense of making a reasoned commitment to a position that is not formally proven true. So what we can prove hinges on what we can believe. We often are inclined to think that proof and faith are opposites: that we can either prove something or believe it. Or if we cannot prove it, all that is left to us is belief; clearly a less desirable option. Actually they are two sides of the same coin; without believing something, no proof can be made. Proving something does not remove the necessity of belief, rather it requires belief. Often we think that proof is the right response to the skeptic. But that won't work. If he is a real skeptic and refuses to accept anything, then nothing can be proven to him.

Explanations and the reasons for them come to rest on judgments that we make about what is an acceptable starting place for our reasoning and object of our commitment. Furthermore, the cognitive subsystems model discussed in the previous chapter suggests that those rational judgments about what assumptions are correct, in turn, depend on intuitive or tacit cognitive and affective processes. They are tacit or intuitive in the sense used in cognitive psychology: that is they often operate in a semiconscious way.

Sometimes when I say these things in class, students respond with outrage that I am saying that we cannot prove anything, maybe even that we cannot know anything. That, of course, is the opposite of what I am saying. I have just discussed how we prove the Pythagorean Theorem or demonstrate the chemical composition of water. I am clear that we can prove the truth of the Pythagorean Theorem; geometry was my favorite subject in tenth grade. I am convinced that under normal conditions here on earth, objects fall according to Newton's inverse square law of gravity. I also do not doubt that George Washington was the first president of the United States. But, of course, I am also saying that we demonstrate these things to be true only in the context of certain fields; by using the axioms of Euclidean geometry, by measuring the rate of descent and formalizing it in calculus, by carefully studying the documents from American history. And doing those things requires accepting and committing ourselves to the axioms, assumptions, and rules of practice that make up geometry, or physics, or historical study.

So I am proposing a three-tiered model of explanation: (1) explicit procedures and reasoning are based on (2) background axioms, assumptions, and procedures that we judge to be proper and to which we commit ourselves, and our acceptance of these assumptions is, in turn, influenced by (3) tacit or intuitive sensibilities about how the world works. That brings us to an obvious question: if we do not demonstrate or prove our background assumptions, if they often result from our tacit or intuitive sensibilities, where does that leave us regarding these basic assumptions and the rules of practice that ground the explanations we give and our reasons for them? That question we will take up in a moment, when we examine the third characteristic of explanations and the reasons for them. This tripartite model will help structure and clarify the coming discussion about where and why I disagree with those who take up cognitive science as a weapon in a crusade against religion.

A second characteristic of explanations and the reasons for them is that they are selective. Some years ago, there was an unfortunate rash of suicides at a nearby university. Over a three-week period, several students jumped from a dormitory balcony. An intense and unhappy discussion about why this happened ensued. The head of the counseling service, whom I happened to know, was called upon to participate in this process. Interviews with friends and families led her to conclude that at least two of the students were severely depressed. Studies show a close connection between suicide and depression and that became her explanation for this tragedy. A sociology professor who studied adolescent group behavior wrote a column in the university newspaper describing a phenomenon he called "copy-cat activity" based on what he called "the epidemiology of group behavior." That is, adolescents tend to follow each other's behavior, whether taste in music or dress or even "acting out" or fatal activities. And it turned out that all these students knew each other and had been talking together about suicide for some time before that horrible three-week period. The head of the university police department weighed in with the results of his investigation that uncovered that several of the students had been drinking in their rooms before they jumped. This was confirmed by toxicology reports of high blood levels of alcohol. In all honesty, they did not ask the head of the physics department for his analysis. But if asked, he could surely claim that as a physicist he was positive that the each body fell from the balcony at a rate consistent with Newton's inverse square law of gravity.

Out of this whole complex tragic episode, each expert would attend to one aspect of the event in his or her explanation: the psychological state of the students, the effect of group dynamics, illegal substance abuse, and the rate of descent of falling bodies. The point here is not who was correct; they all have some supporting evidence. Or which explanation was more important; all these factors clearly played a role. My point is that each explanation required selecting one facet of the tragedy to focus on. And that is characteristic of any process of explanation; it is always selective.

In this case, and in most cases, that selectivity is driven by the frame of reference that a person brings to the subject under investigation. Like schemas discussed in the previous chapter, shared disciplinary frames of reference highlight some aspects of a phenomenon and conceal others. The psychologist focuses on psychopathology; the sociologist on group behavior; the policeman on illegal activity; the physicist on natural law. The sociologist may miss the presence of psychopathology; the psychologist may miss the power of group dynamics; the policeman may overlook both. And probably none of them will have the calculation of the rate of descent of falling bodies on their minds. Each frame of reference enabled each observer to offer one explanation while potentially blinding them to others.

Let me give you a scientific example from my own experience. I am trained in behavioral medicine and psychophysiology; this has been part of my clinical practice for some years and I have taught this material as well. When I first started studying psychology in the 1960s, if someone had applied for a grant to study the impact on health of psychological factors like feelings or beliefs, they would have been ridiculed and maybe even relieved of their tenure. While there were a lot of anecdotal accounts circulating in the clinical world at the time of personality factors being correlated with medical conditions, we were all taught, for example, that the central nervous system (CNS—basically, the brain and spine) and the immune system were totally separate and that the autonomic nervous system, which controls breathing and heart rate, was just that "autonomic," working on its own, uninfluenced by other factors or systems, especially the CNS. That was the frame of reference that kept any scientifically inclined clinician from considering the role of psychological factors in health and disease. One might as well have proposed research on the connection between astrological sign and disease. This was not irrational blindness. There simply was no way, then, of scientifically seeing any possible connections among these physiological systems. Decades of research have now clearly established all sorts of interconnections here through neurological, hormonal, and chemical pathways. And that has made so-called mind-body medicine, or psychoneuroimmunology, a busy field of research and clinical practice. The point is not that researchers and clinicians in the '60s were irrationally close-minded. They were not. The point is that we are all often encapsulated in disciplinary frames of reference and governed by schemas that shed a clear light on some things and inevitably blind us to others. So to reflect critically and constructively on cognitive science and religion, we must become as conscious as we can about what is clearly illuminated and what is inevitably hidden by these explanations.

The third characteristic of explanations and the reasons for them is that they are designed to fulfill very particular functions. If questioned, I cannot provide a formal geometrical proof for geometry as a field. Nor, if questioned, can I provide a laboratory experiment that will demonstrate the truth of the whole field of chemistry. Does that mean that our preferences for these disciplines are irrational; that we cannot give reasons for them? I think not. But the reasons we give will not be the formal proofs found within Euclidean geometry or the result of rule-governed experimental methods like those within chemistry. Rather we will probably point out the ways in which geometry and chemistry are useful to us. We will point to the functions they serve. We will justify them pragmatically.

Put another way, if two people accept the axioms of Euclidean geometry but disagree about a particular claim, say the relationship of angles in a triangle, presumably one can prove to the other which position is correct, based on the rules and axioms of Euclidean geometry which they both accept. But if the dispute is about the axioms themselves, then no compelling proof can be given, since that proof would depend on the axioms in question. Likewise, if two similarly trained chemists disagree about a certain issue, presumably an experiment can be devised to settle the issue, based on the assumptions and procedures of chemistry that they both share. But if the dispute has to do with these assumptions and procedures themselves, with what count as valid data, how much measurement error is allowable, whether all the relevant factors have been included in the experimental design, then it will be much harder, if not impossible, to settle the dispute by an agreed-upon experiment.

In these cases where the basic axioms and procedures that ground an explanatory field are being disputed, compelling proof is not possible, nor is a definitive experiment likely. Instead, judgment is called for, and the discussion will probably revolve around pragmatic or functional issues. Reasons can be given, but they will likely be pragmatic. Which set of axioms does the best explanatory job for geometry? Which assumptions and procedures best help solve the problems that chemistry faces right now? At a more basic level, the criteria for accepting or rejecting a discipline or area of study or outlook on life are probably intuitive in the cognitive science sense discussed earlier. And if these are questioned, the reasons given for them are probably going to be functional and pragmatic as well. Another way to put this is that when agreed-upon procedures and theories are under consideration, then one can logically call for proofs and demonstrations and decisions about the correctness of a claim can rest there. When the background assumptions and the basic frame of reference are at issue, then pragmatic reasons are the only kind that can be given. And the same is true of the even more basic tacit cognitions that motivate the judgments we make about what assumptions to accept or reject.

By "pragmatic" I do not mean a simplistic notion, "if it works, it must be true." Rather, by "pragmatic" I mean two things. First,

that the truthfulness of our most basic, bedrock intuitive outlooks is discovered only by practicing them. The scientist and
philosopher Michael Polanyi says that basic beliefs are "proven
true by committing yourself to them and living them out." I cannot prove to you in some formal way that scientific investigation
will yield new information or that order can be discovered in
nature. You take my word for it or deduce it from articles by science journalists. But the only way you can know it for yourself
is to commit yourself to it and live it out. I cannot prove to you
in some formal way that running or mountain climbing can be
exhilarating. The only way you can know that for yourself is to
commit yourself to doing it. I cannot prove to you in some formal
way that it is more blessed to give than to receive, or that living
a socially connected life is more fulfilling than living an isolated
one. The only way you can know those things is to commit yourself to them and live them out. I cannot prove to you in some formal way that meditation and contemplation can transform your
sense of yourself and the world or that studying sacred texts can
bring new ethical insights or the worship can strengthen moral
commitment. You can just accept the research that supports
such claims. But the only way you know their truth for yourself
is to commit yourself to them and live them out.

Second, by "pragmatic" I refer to what these basic assumptions and axioms allow us to do. Which frame of reference makes
the most sense of our experience, allows us to understand the
widest range of issues, is most closely tied to other positions and
ideas we hold dear, supplies us with the kind of information we
most value. These criteria, which we will discuss in more detail
in chapter 5, are more tacit than those we use at the explicit
level. And the decision about them rests not on proof or demonstration, but on our rational judgment; another point we will
return to in the final chapter.

Three Levels of Explanation: Two Types of Disagreement

These three levels of explanatory discourse mean that such disciplines contain two domains: what we might call, in a not very ingenious way, the "rule-governed" and the "non-rule-governed."

(1) As we said before, there is the rule-governed, explicit domain that contains the overt practices and ideas which we usually think of when we think of a particular field. The proofs and rules of reasoning that make up the practice of geometry. The lab benches and equipment, the periodic table and the theories surrounding it, the computer programs that one finds in a chemistry classroom. Or the sitting meditation postures, the chanting, the sacred scrolls, and the philosophical teachings that one encounters in a Zen monastery. In this domain, questions are being addressed, attempts are made to solve problems, insights and knowledge claims are being generated. The content is radically different in all three contexts—geometry, chemistry, Zen—and so the practices are inevitably radically different as well. Therefore the type of knowledge claimed and insight gleaned are also, of necessity, radically different in all three contexts. But at a very general level, something pragmatic and functional is taking place in all three; they are all trying to accomplish something.

(2) In any field that seeks understanding and explanation, all of its explicit, relatively routinized, question-answering, problem-solving, insight-gaining activity depends upon background assumptions and procedures that are judged correct. Such judgments about basic

assumptions are not formalized or rule-governed but
they are usually conscious and can be discussed.

(3) In addition, as we have said before, there is a more tacit, less
explicit, perhaps even unconscious (unless challenged),
domain of basic, intuitive convictions. This domain too
is not rule-governed. Geometers "feel sure" that space is
implicitly structured in a rational way and that mathematics can explicate that structure. Chemists "just know"
that the substantial world is governed by cause and effect
and these substances can be analyzed into small component parts which will have a clearly discoverable relationship to each other. Zen Buddhists "immediately sense"
that the world of experience is both inevitably in flux and
implicitly interconnected. And the more one practices
these disciplines, the more these sensibilities are usually
strengthened. Such tacit sensibilities appear so obvious
that they do not have to be discussed or even rise into
consciousness. But it is because of these intuitive sensibilities that the field of geometry may be found immediately
appealing to some, that the explicit theories of chemistry
may directly make sense once they are understood, that
the basic teachings of Zen Buddhist may instantly strike
one as insightful and compelling, even before their more
complex dimensions are worked through.

This two-domain model of explanatory disciplines, the overt or
rule-governed and the non-rule-governed background or intuitive domains, enables us to distinguish two types of dispute
about accepting or rejecting explanations. (1) In the case of level
1 above, two or more people may see the world in pretty much the
same way and may accept the same set of claims about it, whether
it is the claims of chemistry or of Zen Buddhism or other variations of scientific and religious discourse. Here the disputants

can refer to the large domain of shared concepts and practices in order to settle the question or solve the problem. Even here, these disputes, either in the sciences or the religions, do not always get settled, but why that is so is beyond the scope of this chapter. My point here is that those kinds of disputes are usually hypothetically resolvable, even if it is not always true in practice.

(2) In the case of non-rule-governed domain, levels (2) and (3) above, disputes usually involve people who do not see the world in the same way regarding the topic under discussion. They do not have the same immediate sensibility there, and so they do not, perhaps cannot, entertain the same set of assumptions about that topic. There is no common tradition of inquiry or practice to call upon here. There is no common frame of reference within which to situate the discussion. There is no common interpretation of the relevant experience or data; and, in some cases, there is no common experience or data at all to appeal to. These discussions do not appear to me to be even hypothetically resolvable. Decisions about the correctness and incorrectness of our background assumptions and intuitive sensibilities rest upon our reflective judgments, which we are responsible for as thinking persons, but not on coercive logical arguments or certain demonstrations.

Does that mean that no discussion is possible or useful here at the more non-rule-governed domain? Certainly not. To repeat a point made earlier, it simply means that one cannot logically call for the same kind of discussion and the same kind of reasoning when these more tacit and implicit areas are the subject than one can expect when it is a discussion among people who experience the world in the same way or belong to the same discipline or field. Such discussions, even if no resolution is expected or possible, can be extremely interesting and fruitful. But the participants must be interested in learning from those they disagree with and in appreciating another's position and the reasons for it, even if they are sure they will never share it.

In the coming pages, I will register both kinds of disagreement with those who seek to use cognitive science to debunk religion. Most of my disagreements with the debunkers' use of cognitive science involve these more fundamental levels of background assumptions and intuitive sensibilities. But there will be a few places where I dispute the "facts" as they present them in support of their antireligious case. These will primarily refer to their "modular" theory of the mind and their reliance on evolutionary psychology and the nature and role of conscious and intentionality. As we shall see, these are themselves highly contested areas in the scientific community, and not only among those involved in the study of religion. In these areas, I do not think the data support the claims of religion's debunkers. And I offer some examples later on. So part of my argument with them is a scientific argument, in which my understanding of the current findings of cognitive science differs from theirs. Eventually the scientific community will decide whether the modular theory of the mind and the framework of evolutionary psychology offer the best accounts of these domains.

Generally I accept the findings generated by the cognitive science of religion. My dispute is usually not with the research but rather with the interpretation of the research on the part of those who seek to use it to debunk religion. And that interpretative dispute most likely derives from different basic assumptions and intuitive sensibilities, and not from disagreements over the "facts."

Disputing Basic Assumptions

Many disputes about cognitive science and religion are driven by different judgments regarding basic assumptions and by even "deeper" intuitive cognitions, the domain that, according to cognitive science, shapes our more explicit and reasoned cognitions in both science and religion and in every field of study. These are usually not disputes about data and experience but rather about the interpretation of data and experience. And these varying interpretations of the same set of facts are driven by the judgments we are willing to make and live by and even by our varying intuitive sensibilities about ourselves and the world. Before we apply this directly to cognitive science and religion, I want to say a little more about this type of disagreement over the interpretation of a common set of research findings or a common set of experiences. They will be our main focus in the coming pages.

A friend of mine, many years ago, recovered in a few days from a serious motorcycle accident that we were told was almost sure to claim his life. The medical resident called it one of those rare medical anomalies that do happen sometime. My friend's church-going family called it a miracle. My point is not to argue the issue of miracles but to use this story to illustrate a point about certain disputes between science and religion. Everyone agreed that the injured friend made an unexpected and normally inexplicably rapid recovery. These "facts" were not in doubt. But two different interpretations were possible depending on one's view of the world. If one's view of the world contained only common, physical causes, all one could reasonably say was that that was an anomaly. A view of the world that contained the possibility of processes or powers beyond common, physical ones makes additional interpretative opportunities available. Whether it is reasonable to hold such a view of the world will be discussed in the next chapter.

A former colleague from the biological sciences described once looking through a microscope at a slide of a cell while on his postdoc, something he had done hundreds and hundreds of times before. In fact he saw nothing there he had not seen before.

There were exactly the same cellular structures he had observed over and over during years of training. But he told me it suddenly struck him that he could not believe that all this complexity was simply the result of randomness and chance operating over very long time periods. That is what he had been taught all his life. He was not, at the time, a religious person or from a religious family. From his first biology class onward, he had always accepted the standard claim that all biological structures and processes originated in a world presided over by randomness and chance. And even after his experience he never rejected that model entirely. But he did come to think that some other, more purposeful agency must also play a role. My point again is not to argue over the science of the origin of life. I have no stake in this issue. Nothing changes for me if the scientific case for a purely random process is compelling or if it is not. I like the story because it is true and it too illustrates my point about differences between science and religion usually being about interpretation, not data. My friend and his colleagues who were appalled at what he was saying all looked through the same microscope and saw the same slide. Again the data were the same; but the interpretation very different.

Such disputes, I suggest, will most likely never be settled simply by appeals to data or experiment, since both sides are looking at the same data. The issue is not at this explicit level. Rather the disagreement is probably over the judgments we make and live by about the nature of things. And these differing judgments may reflect our differing intuitive sensibilities, our most fundamental ways of experiencing our self and our world.

Two more scientific or semi-scientific examples: Suppose we ask, can you remember your birth? This is apparently a straightforward question. There is no doubt that some people, either spontaneously or under hypnosis, produce birth-like memories of trips through tunnels, gasping for breath, soaked in blood, and so on. Some of these are quite compelling. So for most of human history, most believed that, of course, you could remember your birth. But then neurology came along and demonstrated that the newborn's brain was not physiologically developed enough to support such complex memories; the nerves are not myelinated, that is enclosed, enough. So for most people that settled the matter. No birth memories. Anything that sounded like that was the mind's confabulation, like a dream. But wait. That position depends on the assumption that consciousness is totally and completely dependent on the brain. Most scientists insist that is the case. But if you should conclude that consciousness might function apart from the brain, then the fact that the brain is not fully developed would not necessarily be an impediment to memory formation. Once again, my point is not to dispute about birth memories, another issue in which I have no stake. My point is only to argue that one of the things that govern how you come out on this issue is your tacit sense about consciousness's relationship to the brain.

Most physicists agree that the universe is remarkable "fine-tuned"—that is the preferred term—in a way that makes life as we know it possible. If the gravitational pull was only very slightly different from what it is, the universe could not have formed at all. If the bonding properties of carbon were changed by the tiniest degree, carbon-based life could not have happened. Many see this as possible evidence for an intelligent, creative hand at work in the cosmos. Others see it as a very happy coincidence. Again, one last time, how it appears to you is probably governed by your basic assumptions about the world and the process of scientific understanding; and even by your more tacit sensibility about the nature of the reality. For you, is the only reality the physical universe or is some other power also possibly minding the store? Again, the data are not in dispute but rather the interpretation of the data and the judgments we make about it.

So, some disagreements occur among people who share a similar training or outlook or set of convictions about the topic. These are resolvable in principle, and the questions I will soon raise about differing theories of the mind and the fruitfulness of evolutionary psychology are mainly of that kind. Other disagreements occur at the level of fundamental assumptions and the judgments on which they rest. And some occur at the more intuitive, tacit level. Most of my disagreements with religion's debunkers occur in these domains. These are not so likely to be resolvable, unless someone changes their worldview or their intuitive sensibilities shift. Differences in worldviews and our judgments about them, and even our basic intuitions, can still be discussed. But the discussion will not bring forth compelling proofs or convincing arguments, but rather pragmatic and functional concerns and judgments. Now how does all this apply to the explanations of the religion given by cognitive neuroscience?

Explanatory Incompleteness

The three characteristics of explanation described above— background assumptions and their intuitive foundations, selectivity, and particular functions—add up to an important conclusion: all explanations are inevitably incomplete. Two aspects of this incompleteness are important here. First, explanations are selective. No field's explanations can explain everything about a phenomenon. Each field will select only some aspects of a phenomenon to explain; those most relevant to that field's function or most visible in its frame of reference. No single field can or will give a complete account of a particular subject. For example, no single expert gave a complete account of the suicidal tragedies mentioned above. In the coming pages we will probe the cognitive science of religion for possible relevant and important factors that the debunkers ignore in their theorizing and that render their explanations of religion incomplete.

This inevitable incompleteness in our theorizing should generate what I have elsewhere called "epistemic humility," where we acknowledge the limits of the assertions we make and take those limits into account when we discuss our positions with those who disagree with us. Recognizing this inevitable incompleteness in all our accounts, religious and scientific, should constrain us from making exaggerated and grandiose claims on behalf of those accounts. Unfortunately, in the coming pages we will find too many examples of such exaggerations in the current cognitive science of religion.

Second, explanations are inevitably incomplete regarding their starting points and background assumptions. Euclidean geometry has no explanation for its starting axioms. They are just assumed or postulated. Any explanation would have to be in terms of some system or frame of reference beyond Euclidean geometry. Likewise, chemistry cannot explain why the world is made up of substances that make chemical analysis possible and that have the rational structure symbolized in the periodic table. Chemistry can just assume that it does and proceed on that basis. Perhaps that reality could be explained by a deeper theoretical framework like physics. But physics too must begin by assuming the universe has a certain rational structure—even if, in the case of quantum mechanics, it may not be our sense of rationality that is found there and that there are certain constants or symmetries that give the universe the structure that it possesses. This is an incompleteness that is built right into the logic of all of our explanatory structures. Rather than openly acknowledge the assumptions with which they begin and how these assumptions may constrain their theorizing, many in cognitive science often pass over them unacknowledged, or pretend that they are obvious or self-evident. Much of the coming discussion will be devoted to challenging the obviousness and even the rationality of their apparent starting points.

Saying an account is incomplete does not say it is wrong. That would make no sense, since all accounts are incomplete, right or wrong. The physicist's description of the suicides as examples of Newton's law of gravity would certainly not be wrong. But it is obviously wildly incomplete. The linking of the suicides to substance abuse was not wrong; it was attested to by the autopsy reports. But it could not stand on its own as an explanation for their actions. An account can be incomplete and still be correct. As a matter of fact, there is no alternative. Correct accounts are still incomplete.

Explanatory Incompleteness in CSR: A Question of Method

There are two additional ways in which the findings of cognitive science in relation to religion might be seen as incomplete. They go beyond their logical incompleteness and are the result of the particular methodology and a particular model of developmental psychology employed there. Both methodological and developmental incompleteness apply to virtually all current cognitive science explanations of religion, regardless of how they are interpreted. First, the methodology employed often involves breaking religion down into its component parts. In one sense this is simply the method followed in most all the natural sciences. Chemistry involves breaking down (that is what the Greek word "analysis" means) compounds into their component parts: water into hydrogen and oxygen, salt into sodium and chloride. So cognitive science analyzes religion as a compound of beliefs about supernatural agents, teleological causes, nonphysical souls, and so on. Each is referred to a separate cognitive module. Fair enough for the purposes of investigation. Something is gained: knowledge about the component processes. But something is also lost. In the actual lived life of religion, all these components fit together and work together to produce a lived experience that is not simply all these fragments occurring side by side. The gestalt that is the life of religion, which is more than just a list of its cognitive components, gets overlooked in this analysis.

My claim that understanding a phenomenon only by breaking it apart has serious limitations is not an unusual claim even in the physical sciences. Water clearly has properties that isolated atoms of hydrogen and oxygen lack. Salt clearly has properties that individual sodium and chloride atoms could not possess. Nor could these properties be predicted from the nature of the individual component atoms if we did not know the properties of water or salt beforehand. While there is a lot of current discussion in the scientific and philosophical literature about what is called "emergence," what I have said here is not really controversial in natural science. Everyone virtually agrees that interacting systems have properties their components sitting side by side lack. So there is no reason not to think that religion has properties that go beyond its individual cognitive components.

Maybe the realm of human psychology is different? I don't see why. If you ask me why I enjoy my work, I can list a series of components. I enjoy the challenge of the diagnostic detective work of behavior medicine, which, judging by discussions with physician colleagues, often goes beyond the intellectual challenges involved in some mainstream medical practices. I get energized by the psychic arm-wrestling between patient and doctor in intensive psychotherapy. There is the intellectual stimulation that comes from teaching about these matters and from reading professional articles and attending professional conferences. I enjoy the sense of being helpful to people who are suffering. And I am usually well paid for what I do. But none of these things taken separately or just listed like this, completely captures the experience of practicing clinical psychology. They sum up together into something that exceeds the description of these components.

Boyer, in a 2008 article, calls this claim that religion may be more than the sum of its parts "Pure advertising." That statement is pure rhetoric. No direct evidence is provided. No logical argument is proposed. Instead Boyer refers to the module theory of the mind. He says, "these domains [that make up religion] remain separated in human cognition." As we noted in the last chapter, the claim of radical modular separation at the neurological and cognitive levels is highly contested. Boyer's claim that these modules are separated in such a way that the gestalt of religion cannot possess properties beyond those of its individual cognitive components would seem to require a degree of modular autonomy that goes far beyond what is currently held to be the case in cognitive science. If modules were that distinct in the domain of religion, then presumably that would be true in most other domains of human experience. Then the whole question of how the unity of human experience arises, which bedeviled earlier radically modular theories, would arise again in a more radical way. So to make this convincing we need an argument to show that religion is different here from other domains of experience, so that its experienced unity is only an illusion brought about by self-promotion; or we need an argument to show that all unity of experience is an illusion; a hard case to make, to put it mildly.

Boyer's argument here, and much of the writing in the cognitive science of religion, identifies "scientific explanation" only with claims about underlying mechanisms. That is certainly a type of scientific explanation, and it should not be neglected, but this is much too narrow to be considered a complete account of what can be called scientific, given the rise of nonlinear models, paradigms of emergent properties, and nonreductive approaches within science. Today, fundamental physics, biology, organizational theory, nonlinear dynamics, and neurology all rely on scientific models that study an interacting system's holistic and emergent properties. There is no logical or scientific reason to confine one's explanation of religion only to religion's separate cognitive components and to ignore the ways in which these components may also interact and produce a phenomenon richer and more complex than the component parts in isolation. Continuing to rely so exclusively on a singularly modular model gives these theories of religion from cognitive science a slightly outdated ring.

Boyer's discussion here is a projection onto religion of a radical and probably outdated modular theory. This may tell us more about the method than about the phenomenon of religion itself. If you start from a radically modular assumption for your definition of religion as an object of study, you cannot then use it to argue that religion is simply and purely its component parts. You assumed that as a necessary part of studying religion in this way. You have simply confused your conclusion with your premise.

This is clear in one of the best brief discussions of this material in a 2010 paper by Scott Atran and Joseph Henrich. Besides its clarity and conciseness, this article is notable for several additional reasons. The authors appear to recognize that many of their claims are conjectural. Rather than projecting certainty, the authors frequently use the word "may" in making claims, that is, evolution "may" favor X; or beliefs in supernatural agents "may" assist culture in Y ways. Also they sometimes recognize that religion is more than belief in a few "counterintuitive" propositions but also involves extensive and complex cultural practices. Their goal is not "explaining religion" in some grand way but rather a more limited and therefore potentially realizable goal of accounting for religion's prosocial effects. But to do this, they have chosen to go back to the beginning and give an account of the origin of religion itself. Their account reprises the standard cognitive science of religion claims about HADDs and counterintuitve representations giving rise to beliefs in supernatural agents. However, they recognize that there is more to religion than only such beliefs. And those additional aspects of religion require postulating processes beyond a few simple cognitive modules. Thus the article's lengthly subtitle: "How cognitive by-products, adaptive learning heuristics, ritual displays, and group competition generate deep commitments to prosocial religions." The authors are obviously reaching for a more complex model, presumably out of a recognition that religion is a more complex phenomenon than simply a loose collection of beliefs about gods, souls, and spirits. Thus reference to a few cognitive structures is probably not sufficient to do explanatory justice to the world's religions. This implicit recognition is clearly a gain for the scientific study of religion.

The problem is that there is no suggestion that all these rather heuristically isolated phenomena sum up to something that goes beyond a list of the individual processes. This illustrates what I take as a major weakness in many cognitive science accounts of religion. The various factors—"cognitive by-products, adaptive learning heuristics, . . ." etc.—are simply listed and discussed in a rather linear fashion. The result is a rather simple model; perhaps too simple for the domain under consideration. Adding more variables does not automatically make a model more complex. A more complex model requires that the variables are theorized so that they mutually interact and also become integrated in a fashion that produces a richer, more dynamic, and systematic reality than the individual variables taken separately.

A clinical illustration: A young man of junior high school age is referred to a therapist by the courts because of his history of setting fires at home and on school property. The therapist might treat him individually and undertake various interventions to help him understand his motivations better, and so find better solutions to the conflicts he experiences; or to help him access the anger that is propelling him to act out in this way; or to find ways to reinforce more prosocial behavior. On the other hand, the therapist might see him together with his family. In that context the therapist might notice that the young man becomes anxious and fidgety whenever the subject of his father's business trips comes up. The therapist also notices that at those times his mother makes some caring gesture toward his younger sister, asking if she's cold or hungry, for example. In response the younger sister starts to cry unconsolably. So the therapist asks to meet with the parents alone, not even involving the boy who is the target patient. What is she doing? The therapist is treating the family as a single, complex system of mutually interacting members, rather than as a set of individuals with their own private motivations, feelings, and conflicts. Now the therapist learns that when the father goes on his business trips, he stays with a mistress in another city. The parents are discussing divorce but they maintain that the children have no idea about this. Yet whenever a business trip looms, the son lights a fire, the mother reaches out to her daughter for solace, and the daughter has a crying fit. The fires call attention to the existence of a problem and often force the father to come home early to deal with the authorities. The daughter's fits deflect attention away from her brother whom she feels close to and who she fears will get into so much trouble that he will be taken away. The point is that there are patterns—fire starting, overly close mother-daughter bonds, exaggerated crying fits—that emerge and become comprehensible only at a systemic level. Such patterns would never become fully comprehensible by focusing only on the thoughts, feelings, motivations, and behaviors of the individuals involved. These more complex, interacting realities require a more complex level of analysis. My point is that the religiously lived life is more complex than simply an amalgamation of cognitive modules, counterintuitive beliefs, and socially compelling rituals. Those may well all play some part, but a comprehensive account of religion may well require much more complex models than simple lists of atomistically understood individual processes. There is no suggestion in Atran and Henrich's article that all these rather heuristically isolated processes working together would possibly produce something beyond these individual processes studied separately. So the extent of the explanatory reach of a list of separate variables and processes remains questionable.

Atran and Henrich's discussion also underscores the functional nature of much of the cognitive science approach to religion. Their article is basically a list of various possible cognitive and cultural functions that religion performs. One question I am addressing in this book is the extent to which such cognitive evolutionary accounts might undermine the veracity of religious beliefs. Of course, functional accounts have little causal explanatory value, and inevitably the authors deny that religion arose in order to accomplish those things. The function that a set of claims performs, by itself, says nothing about the truth or falsity of those claims. Belief systems considered false may function well, at least for a time. Ptolemaic astronomy predicted eclipses. Marxism and Maoism produced social cohesion and a sense of belonging. I suspect that is what Atran and Henrich think about religion. Its claims are false but its effects can be prosocial. On the other hand, if a set of beliefs does perform the functions it was designed for, that certainly counts in favor of its truthfulness. By itself that may not be decisive, but performing well certainly does not detract from truthfulness. The point is that functional accounts by themselves are no threat to the possible truth claims of religion, especially when they suggest that religion performs positive functions. And that is true of those evolutionary cognitive science accounts of religion that are primarily functional in nature. However, many evolutionary cognitive accounts go beyond a purely functional analysis and claim to undercover the true cause or source of religious belief. That is another matter.

And we should not forget the ways in which all schemas show us some things and conceal others. You might analyze a painting into the chemical formulae for various pigments plus the composition of canvas and the interaction with the physical structure of brushes. If that's all you do, you don't notice that all those separate pigments compose the *Mona Lisa* or Picasso's *Guernica*. Does anyone deny that something more complex than the separate chemical pigments emerges? Likewise, it is not irrational to suggest that the life of religion may emerge from the summing up of its cognitive substructures into something more complex and illuminating. Something missed if those cognitive substructures are the sole focus of attention.

I am not disputing here the claim that cognitive processes like agency detection and tendencies toward anthropomorphic and teleological thinking play a role in religion. I am disputing that reference to such factors, especially when treated in isolation, as current cognitive evolutionary psychology grounded in a massively modular model requires, can get us very far in explaining the complexity and diversity of religious beliefs and practices. I am sure these processes play a role. I have not seen any evidence that it is a very large role. Robert McCauley recognizes this when he says, in reference to his own cognitive account of religion "an analysis of the cognitive naturalness of religion . . . does not provide a comprehensive theory of religious cognition, let alone a comprehensive theory of religion."

Explanatory Incompleteness in CSR: A Question of Development

A second additional incompleteness involved in much of the current attempts to explain religion by cognitive science involves its use of developmental psychology. Much of the actual research relied on in cognitive psychology's theories of the origin of religion is referred to as coming from developmental psychology. But mostly it is infant and early-childhood research. This is a very truncated understanding of development from the perspective of someone like myself who approaches and teaches developmental research from a clinical framework. A clinical framework requires a life-span approach, since patients of all ages show up in the doctor's office. This virtual limitation of "development" to infancy and early childhood does mischief when the studies are applied to religion. The implicit message is that religion is childish; that one can jump directly from the child's personification of her teddy bear or his insistence on living in a teleological universe to the *Summa Theologiae* or the *Avatamsaka Sutra* or the *Upanishads* with no cognitive development in between.

Of course that is not what life-span developmental research actually finds. Rather, decades of research on cognitive development in moral and religious domains find clear trajectories of development toward more cognitive complexity and more encompassing rationalities within religious and moral development. The highest and most complex forms of cognition can be found as often in the domain of religion as in other domains. Current research finds very little difference in average levels of cognitive complexity in the reasoning of religious believers and nonreligious skeptics. Science may begin from the young child's incessant demand to know "why" and her early grasp of number and grouping. But science develops into something richer and more complex and enlightening through disciplined processes of research and reflection. Likewise, religion may begin from a child seeing faces in a cloud and distinguishing naturally occurring from manufactured objects. But religion develops into something much richer and more complex and enlightening, if practiced through disciplined contemplation and critical philosophical reflection. This is apparent in the histories of Plato and Plotinus, of the Upanishadic and Vedantic philosophies of Hinduism, of the Mahayana and Vajrayana Buddhist traditions, of Patristic and Medieval Christian thought and of Medieval Muslim literature. All of them show trajectories of increasingly sophisticated and complex forms of reasoning taking place within various religions. It is a paradoxical theory of religious development in which no actual development is seen to take place. That single-minded focus on the beliefs of children obscures the cognitive development that does take place in the domain of religion.

Once again Boyer simply engages in special pleading in order to rid his theory of evidence that doesn't fit. He suggests, without providing any evidence, that more complex forms of religious reflection are special cases, not part of common, ordinary religious practices, and so can simply be disregarded when seeking to understand religion. Because they are supposedly really determined by unconscious cognitive processes "theologies, explicit dogmas, scholarly interpretations of religion cannot be taken as reliable descriptions of either the contents or causes of people's religious beliefs," Boyer writes. This, of course, is another place where cognitive science of religion mirrors exactly the psychoanalysis of religion claims and debates of fifty years ago. Like Freud, once again we cherry-pick the examples that fit our explanations, in this case children's religion and our ancestor's hypothetical religious beliefs and practices, and disregard what doesn't fit, the more complex religious practices and beliefs. That was not appropriate scientific method in Freud's day, for which he was roundly and appropriately criticized, and it is not good practice in our day either. But even there the cherry-picked evidence may not support their case. Day writes, "Whenever we scratch the surface of the anthropological record and look a little more closely, the religious systems we discover are rarely the minimalist affairs of modestly counter-intuitive, easily acquired concepts that the cognitive optimum hypothesis forecasts." And in the next chapter, when considering evolutionary explanations, we will look at more evidence that suggests that rather complex forms of religion were present among our earliest ancestors. So complexity in religion may not be so easily swept under the rug.

So beyond the logical incompleteness and selectivity that characterize all explanations, cognitive science explanations of religion may contain additional incompleteness as a result of their singularly, and perhaps passé, modular methods and their lack of attention to religious cognitive development beyond childhood. I hope it is clear that incompleteness is not a synonym for false. Both true and false accounts are still logically incomplete. But realizing the inevitable incompleteness of any single system of explanations should generate the following cautions. (1) In looking at the explanations of religion provided by cognitive science, even if they are correct, we should beware if they explicitly or implicitly claim a completeness of explanation that logically they cannot possess. (2) We should both appreciate what they tell us about religion and be alert to what they, of necessity, fail to notice or to include in their accounts. (3) We should look into the implicit, tacit affects and cognitions that drive their interpretations and what constitutes the background against which their arguments are constructed and appear compelling.

We might also remember that none of these claims are really new or original. We have already remarked on many parallels with Freud's theorizing, and we will do so again. Like Freud and the CSR, many of the nineteenth-century founders of the field of religious studies felt that the primary way to understand religion was by understanding its origins. Müller, Tyler, and Fraser all thought the essence of religion was to be found in its earliest and most primitive forms. Tyler, for example, learned what he could about so-called primitive tribes on the assumption that their "religious" beliefs and practices represented the earliest and most foundational religious forms. He claimed that most primitive religion was "animism;" that is the belief that "spirits" inhabited the physical world. This, he argued, represented the tendency of primitive mentality to personify everything and to explain all occurrences as the actions of personal agency. He was convinced that this entailed that science would soon replace religion. Religion, by his definition, was explanation by personal agency; science was explanation by impersonal, mechanical causality. The assumption was that both religion and science functioned as "explanations." But obviously science was more accurate. Muller, Tyler, and Fraser all agreed that science and religion perform parallel functions, so religion is just a prescientific attempt at explanation. Eventually it will be replaced by science, which is much better at it.

It is not clear exactly how much explanatory power we achieve by understanding the historical origin of a human phenomenon. Freud has been roundly criticized for committing the "genetic fallacy," that is claiming to have found the origin of religion in a primal act of Oedipal patricide (Freud's account of the genesis of religion in his book *Totem and Taboo*) and then arguing Oedipal dynamics are the key to religion; an argument no one, even psychoanalysts, accepts today. That was considered a logical fallacy because the origin of a belief or a behavior casts little light on its truthfulness. Chemistry has clear historical roots in alchemy; yet contemporary chemistry is not simply alchemy in modern form. Astronomy has clear historical roots in astrology, yet contemporary cosmology is far from a variant form of astrology. Likewise, Tyler's theory of religion as essentially animism was soon dismissed by philosophers and historians of religion. Even if it were true that our Paleolithic ancestors were animists, that entails nothing about contemporary Zen Buddhism, Islam, or any other religion.

These assertions by early scholars that the best way to understand religion is by finding its origins, and that religion is basically a primitive form of explanation, probably by relying on personified powers, echo again in much current cognitive science of religion. I have often heard cognitive scientists of religion complain that people in religious studies and the humanities in general ignore, or even fear, their findings. Perhaps. But maybe historians and philosophers of religion think they have heard it all before, and that arguments based on theories of origin or descriptions of religion as primitive science were unconvincing in the nineteenth century and remain so today.

How the Conclusion Came to Exceed the Argument

The crusaders or debunkers—the focus of this book—claim that cognitive science heralds the demise of religion, all religion. They interpret, in their own particular way, the findings of cognitive science that suggest that religious beliefs utilize common cognitive processes like pattern recognition, attributions of causality, perceptions of others' minds, etc. For example, it is almost universally asserted that such findings prove that religion is a purely natural phenomenon. Clearly these findings do no such thing. All they suggest is that natural, human processes are at work in religion, something virtually no one denies. That does not logically entail that *only* natural processes are present, rather it simply entails that some of the processes involved in religion are natural. If it should be the case, and I am not arguing that it is the case, that some nonnatural processes were also at work in the development of a religious outlook, a purely naturalistic method would never find them. Remember that schemas and frames of reference allow us to see things and blind us to others. I have already stated clearly that as a psychologist of religion, I certainly think that religion is a human phenomenon. I am not arguing otherwise here. I am just pointing to this claim as one example, and there will be others, of the interpretative overreach often at work in this discussion. Cognitive science finds common human cognitive processes are at work in religion. That's all.

Of course it adds to our knowledge in important ways by elaborating what some of those processes might be. But logically it does not go beyond that to eliminate all other possible factors. The debunkers seem to be assuming that if natural processes are at work, nothing else can be. But no argument is offered to support that assumption. In chapter 4 I argue at length that that assumption is seriously mistaken and also suggest some reasons why the debunkers feel, wrongly I think, that no arguments are needed to support it. It is just intuitively obvious to them. But aren't we supposed to be skeptical about ideas that appear intuitively obvious? Or does that rule apply only to religious intuitions and not the intuitions that undergird the beliefs of the debunkers? Why that double standard? More about that in a moment. Why the assumption that there must be only one set of causes or influences at work in the world? Isn't the world complex enough to contain a plurality of influences? Can we not count beyond one?

Such findings cannot be used to prove, in a strong sense, that religion is simply a natural phenomenon. Rather, these findings assume that religion is a natural phenomenon. Such an assumption is basic to any scientific study of religion. Any psychological study of religion must begin from that assumption; otherwise religion could not be an object of scientific investigation. But having started by assuming that religion is a natural phenomenon, one cannot then turn around and say that the cognitive science of religion proves it. To argue that way, again, is to mistake conclusion for premise.

In addition, there is a serious question about whether physicalist explanations make all other accounts necessarily irrational or unconvincing. Justin Barrett argues at length that there is no logical or necessary reason to always prefer physicalist explanations and that providing such explanations does not logically or necessarily vitiate religious claims. Clark and Barrett state the obvious when they write, "Showing that natural causes are involved in the production of a belief tells us nothing about the truth or falsity of that belief. ... Both natural and supernatural explanations may be true." So one logical problem with the debunkers' argument is that describing one set of processes at work in a phenomenon like religion does not automatically cancel out there being other factors also at work. At least argument or evidence is necessary to show why other factors cannot also be involved. None are forthcoming here.

In addition, suggesting that uncovering the psychological causes or motivations for religious beliefs automatically implies that such beliefs are false is a serious logical error.

The assumption here is that demonstrating the evolutionary origin of our beliefs undermines their truth. Freud made the same mistake. As the atheist philosopher J. L. Mackie, after a long survey of such arguments puts it, "even an adequate, unified natural history which incorporated all these factors would not in itself amount to a disproof of theism ... no account of the origin of a belief can settle the question of whether that belief is true or not." This point has generated a lot of discussion, in part because of the application of evolutionary psychology to morality and religion. But the consensus supports the argument made here, that, as Guy Kahane writes, "obviously, the mere fact that there is a causal explanation of a belief does nothing to effect its justification. All beliefs have a causal explanation."

So finding causes for beliefs entails little or nothing about the correctness of those beliefs. All beliefs have psychological and neurological causes. But there is an additional issue beyond whether religious beliefs are correct, and that is whether or not religious beliefs can be justified. Here, the debunkers appear to insist that when a person learns the possible natural causes of their religious belief, that belief (hypothetically correct or not) is no longer justified. They seem to suggest that if a religious belief is naturally caused, it cannot be true. That appears to assume that for religious beliefs to be true, or to be truly religious, they must not be caused naturally. To my knowledge the debunkers present no reasons to support such an assumption. There may be some religious people who do believe that. But religious people are under no obligation to believe that. There is no logical or theological reason why religious beliefs cannot have natural causes. Most theists believe God works through natural causes; and many religious people who are not theists, Buddhists and Hindus for example, believe that natural human reason, when properly trained, can discover religious truth. Finding out that natural faculties play a role in forming a religious belief does not necessarily undermine the justification for that belief.

But there is a deeper issue here. Supposing it could be shown that because of the operation of HADDs and other natural human cognitive processes, a person would inevitably believe in God, even if there was no justification for belief in God. It is clear that natural human cognitive processes do not inevitably produce belief in God. The growing number of atheists is strong evidence against that claim. So it is not the case that these cognitive processes inevitably make people into theists. The power of these natural human cognitive processes is not so great that belief in God is immune from falsification or insensitive to the presence of disconfirming arguments. So it is simply not the case that because of these cognitive processes, people are compelled to believe in God. Therefore it is not the case that people must believe in God even if they have no reasons or justifications to believe in God. Some people may, but that is not inevitable.

The debunkers want a believer to think that, because of their cognitive processes, they would have believed in God even if there were no justification for belief in God. But knowing I could be wrong is not usually taken as a reason not to believe that I am right. Saying I should not believe anything if I can imagine that I might be wrong sets the bar for justified belief way too high. If the history of philosophy shows nothing else, it shows that almost any belief can be reasonably doubted. Hypothetically, I could read the writings of the eighteenth-century British philosopher David Hume and start to doubt my belief in causality. Knowing that my belief in causality could be wrong does not undermine the justifications I think I have for that belief. The fact that I believe it, even while knowing that it could (at least hypothetically) be wrong, does not make my belief in causality unjustified. Likewise, the thoughtful theist, Buddhist, or Hindu does not lose their justifications for their beliefs if they recognize they might be mistaken. The only alternative would be a radical skepticism that says no beliefs are truly justified since virtually all beliefs can be doubted and therefore might be believed even if wrong. But cognitive scientists are clearly not radical skeptics. And if they deploy arguments with radically skeptical premises, they simply undermine their own position.

There is another form of this argument. It says that cognitive science shows that a person's belief in God arises from processes that do not refer to the actual existence of God, and so are independent of the actual existence of God. Again, the assumptions here are that these cognitive processes evolved only to serve reproductive fitness and not to support belief in God and that they are the only source for belief in God. I believe my friend Robert has a sister Ann because he told me. This is surely justified grounds for belief in Ann's sibling relationship to Robert. But that justification makes no reference to whether Ann actually is Robert's sister. She might be his mistress and he wants to disguise his affair by telling me she's his sister. To actually undercut my justification in believing Ann really is Robert's sibling, I would have to go back through the town birth records and see if there was any reference to Ann and Robert here. So the actual debunking point must be that the *final* or *most basic* source for my belief makes no reference to or has no actual relationship to the subject of that belief.

Now it is not clear how that is supposed to work in the case of belief in God. Presumably people who believe in God believe that God is the final or ultimate source of that belief. They may claim that God uses natural causes to bring that belief about. The debunkers are giving a naturalistic account of the origin of belief. For them, natural processes are the final or ultimate source of the belief. But by definition, naturalistic theories make no reference to God. So the fact that they don't in this case is just another way of saying they are naturalistic. The religious person is not blocked from still saying that God's activity is the final or ultimate source of their belief. The only way to block that move is to demonstrate that naturalism is undoubtedly true. That is not likely. So for religious people, their beliefs are the result of God's activity and God is their final and ultimate source, directly or indirectly, even if natural cognitive processes are proximate sources. The naturalistic debunker rejects this and says their final source is in the natural processes alone. But that is just to say that the religious person and the reductive naturalist disagree about naturalism. No big surprise there.

In addition, the insistence that there must be a causal link between the source of a belief and the object of the belief may not be universally valid or necessary. Such an insistence can make it hard to understand how we can justify beliefs about the nature of mathematical objects or universal truths that are not usually regarded as directly causally active. So the requirement of a direct causal connection between belief in God and God may not be a problem for the person who believes in God or may not make sense or be required in the case of belief in God.

Suppose we assume that these cognitive processes alone generate a person's belief in God, an assumption I think is incorrect, but I start there for the sake of argument. The form of the argument would be the same if you started from neuronal firings in the brain. Suppose it is demonstrated to me in the laboratory or the brain scanner that those physical processes are the only reason a person believes as they do. All reasoning is just ex post facto rationalization. Then the religious person is in trouble. All her beliefs are only the result of random or accidental cognitive or neurological conditions. All justification fails. But clearly the same applies to the atheist and the skeptic. Their beliefs too are just the result of their unconscious and accidental cognitive or neurological processes. All their carefully contrived arguments against religious belief are just ex post facto rationalization.

Obviously the debunking cognitive scientist does not believe that. She writes papers trying to convince religious people to see things her way. That would make no sense if she really believed that all beliefs, and that must include beliefs about the veracity of cognitive science or neurology and its deterministic influence on these very same beliefs, are solely the result of deterministic cognitive or neurological dynamics. Obviously the atheistic cognitive scientist believes people can reason about religion and hopefully come to same conclusion she does. The point is that even if it is demonstrated that beliefs simply arise from the operation of implicit cognitive or neurological processes, once the beliefs arise, they can be the subject of rational reflection and discussion. It is completely conceivable that natural processes generate religious cognitions that can then be the subject of cogent reflection and justification. To say otherwise is to undermine all reasoning, even the reasoning that produced the cognitive claims about the origin of religious belief. So even if it is demonstrated that religious beliefs are produced in the way the debunking cognitive scientist says, that does not automatically remove the possibility of justified belief.

In addition, I may at first acquire a belief in an unusually unreliable way. For example, a grade school classmate told me a rumor about a bizarre historical event, a past murder in our town. I didn't believe him. Later I used the usually reliable method of careful investigation and rational reflection and discovered the evidence that such a thing had happened was not coercively convincing, but was pretty good. So even if I acquire a belief in an unusually unreliable way, rumors in elementary school, I can use reliable methods later to produce a sounder grounding for my claims. Likewise a child might "naturally" feel there is a God. In adulthood they may study religion and other fields like philosophy, psychology, or natural science, and through rational reflection come to think that indeed a God or some spiritual power most likely exists. In all these ways, the causes of a belief do not necessarily undermine its truthfulness. That must be assessed on other grounds.

The cognitive science of religion uncovers the common cognitive processes at work in religion. The debunkers deploy these findings as part of a particular *rhetorical* strategy. For example, in a 2003 article, Jesse Bering refers to religion's reliance on our cognitive processes as "pirating aspects of human cognition" and as a "parasite" on human cognition, and then labels religion as an "epidemic." Religion as theft and illness! In a 2008 article, Boyer repeatedly describes religion's reliance on cognition in this way: "religious concepts and activities hijack our cognitive resources." Hijack?! These metaphors certainly make religion sound nefarious: terrorists hijack planes, robbers hijack cars, pirates rape and pillage, epidemics kill. But all cognitive science really suggests is that, like all human activities, religion utilizes our cognitive resources. Nothing nefarious or symptomatic there.

This is a perplexing move. Cognitive science suggests that religion relies on human cognition. What else could it rely on? But then almost immediately the results of human cognition in the domain of religion are redescribed not just as natural, but as mistaken, or worse. In a December 2005 article in *The Atlantic*, Paul Bloom speaks of cognition going "awry" when it comes to religion. He quotes Boyer approvingly when he claims that religion is a "hypertrophy" (abnormal enlargement) of the cognitive system; again an illness metaphor. At a conference, I recently heard a lecture on this topic, in which neurons were spoken of as "misfiring" in the case of religion. Without missing a beat, the debunkers move from religion as natural to religion as always wrong and often pathological.

How is the rhetorical sleight of hand accomplished? Not by evidence or argument. No arguments or evidence are offered to show that claims about supernatural agents are always and everywhere mistaken or that religion is closely connected with psychopathology. All the epidemiological research finds just the reverse. All that is offered here is that religious beliefs and practices arise from the functioning of normal human cognition. Nor could the findings of cognitive science, which deals with how human cognition works and not with the question of what actually exists in reality, ever demonstrate that claims about supernatural realities are always and everywhere false. That's clearly far beyond the purview of research into the functioning of schemas and the movement of neurotransmitters.

Rather I would suggest that what makes this rhetorical sleight of hand work is the "background" or context in which the debunkers deploy the relatively neutral scientific findings of cognitive research. They appear to simply assume that all religious claims are always mistaken and that virtually every religious practice is cognitively pathological. They don't have to demonstrate it or give reasons for it. That conviction is just intuitively obvious to them. And in what context does such a belief appear intuitively obvious? Most likely one in which it is assumed that science is the only arbiter of knowledge and that the only reality is what is disclosed to us through natural science. The debunkers do not have to argue for this stance or give reasons for it. It is intuitively obvious. It is simply the background against which they write and the context in which they conduct their discussion.

After rhetorically labeling religion's use of human cognition as a criminal activity ("hijacking"), Boyer adds "as do music, visual art, cuisine, politics, economic institutions and fashion." What is missing from this list? Science! Surely science too relies on ("hijacks"?) human cognition. Cognitive science is no different from any other human activity in terms of its dependence on human cognition. Robert McCauley writes, "Science calls upon some cognitive processes that come to humans relatively easily. Humans are naturals at thinking of theories, and they are sensitive to kinds of evidence that bear on those theories' truth. . . . I grant freely that not all aspects of scientific thought are cognitively unnatural." Despite this, over and over we will find this same rhetorical strategy among the debunkers, uncritically granting science an epistemological privilege *carte blanche*. In the next chapter we will investigate in what sense that tactic might or might not be justified.

For example, after arguing that the belief in consciousness as existing apart from the body results when our cognitive system "overshoots" and so infers things that do not really exist, in his *Atlantic* article Bloom addresses the obvious question of how we know that belief represents an "overshooting" and overinferring of cognition. He offers no evidence or argument to support his assumption that such a claim is mistaken. Rather, he simply appeals to authority. Such a notion, he tells us, "clashes starkly with the scientific view." No discussion is offered about the sense in which that asserted "clash" might be correct; rather it is just baldly stated. But Bloom immediately realizes that his cognitive system has overshot and he says, correctly, "I don't want to overstate the consensus here; there is no accepted theory" of how consciousness arises. I much appreciate this attempt at nuancing a rather large, overly general claim on this very complex topic. And my point here is not to take up the "mind-body" problem. I only want to point out that, for Bloom, an appeal to "the scientific view," as he understands it, should close the case; no further reasoning or critical analysis is required.

This same appeal to scientific authority occurred earlier in Bloom's article. In reflecting on the "embarrassment" that so many people still believe in God, Bloom notes that even scientists believe in God in large numbers. No help there for what appears to me to be his implicit case for the irrationality religion.

So he restricts his search to the National Academy of Science. It is not an accepted research practice to restrict your sample to the group that gives you the result you want. There he states, "Only when we look at the most elite scientists ... do we find a strong majority of atheists and agnostics." What is this claim, which I do not dispute, supposed to show? Again it seems to me to be a clear appeal to authority. "Elite scientists" are the arbiters of rationality and truth. I thought rational people were supposed to be critical of authorities, whether religious, political, or scientific. But it seems that for the crusaders against religion, only religious sources are to be treated skeptically. Elite scientific authority is to be accepted without question, even when it is being cited in areas far beyond its domain of competence, like the existence of God. In the world of the debunkers, "elite" science gets an epistemological privilege *carte blanche*.

Religion Is Natural, Science Is Not

This wide-ranging epistemological privilege, going far beyond the research specializations of the particular natural sciences, is expressed clearly when Boyer concludes his article by asserting that "religious thinking seems to be the path of least resistance for our cognitive system. By contrast, disbelief is generally the result of deliberate, effortful work." This contrast of "religion as natural, science as unnatural," to quote the title of Robert McCauley's oft-cited article and book, runs throughout the writings of the crusaders. But in his 2011 book McCauley is clear that by religion he will mean only *popular* religion. "Popular" is almost always italicized in the text to underscore this point. He is not primarily addressing theology or other critical and reflective religious projects but rather "the cognitive status of *popular* understandings about religious belief." Popular religion comes naturally to human beings, or so the argument goes. Popular religion is the direct expression of what McCauley calls "maturationally natural cognitions." These are the "(similar) immediate, intuitive views that pop into mind in domains where they [*homo sapiens*] may have had little or no experience and no instruction." While he wisely sidesteps the issue of whether such cognitions are in some sense "innate," he strongly insists that they are common to the species, not attributable to culture or training, occur spontaneously in young children, and primarily operate unconsciously.

The key to the argument is the insistence that "Religion in its popular, that is, widespread forms . . . employs ideas and forms of thought that are *naturally appealing* to the human mind . . . [and] are available to most children by the time they reach school age." Being simply the direct result of humans' virtually inbred, "maturationally natural" cognitions accounts for religion's appeal. "What makes representations cognitively and psychologically appealing, constitutes the primary selection forces here. . . . Just as humans find some foods particularly good to eat, they find some representations particularly good to think. Religions, like Rube Goldberg devices, tend to capture and enthrall human minds." Religion, then, comes naturally to human beings, not in the sense that there is a "religious gene" or a "God spot" in the brain, but rather that our natural cognitive predispositions drive us to think in religious ways and make us "cognitively ready to leap at, swallow and digest religious stories, actions, symbols, and settings like a hungry frog will leap at, swallow, and (attempt to) digest a ball bearing that flies within reach of its visual field." So the main, perhaps only, reason people hold "popular" religious convictions about transcendent agency is because such ideas "capture and enthrall human minds." No evidence or argument is offered for this assertion. An implication would seem to be that when an adult believer gives thought-out reasons for her beliefs, these reasons are mainly rationalizations for the precipitants of implicit, unconscious cognitive tendencies. A person not familiar with the field of evolutionary cognitive psychology would want some evidence or argument to support a claim about whether, or how much, these natural cognitive proclivities play a role in adult religious life. None is provided here.

The maturationally natural cognition that religion primarily relies on, according to McCauley, is our propensity to see the world in terms of intentional agents. And religions, at least "popular" religions, "rely overwhelmingly on representations about the states of mind and actions of *agents*." But this is a cognitive mistake. Such claims "are often the results of cognitive false alarms." "Often" is an ambiguous word here. We have seen that research finds a human propensity to attribute intentional agency to ambiguous stimuli, especially when subjects are prompted in that direction. How often this is a "false alarm" in real life, as opposed to specifically contrived experimental situations, is not really demonstrated, but is simply asserted, a point we will return to. Usually, in ordinary life, we readily recognize and dismiss such false alarms. I may reflexively talk to, curse at, my computer when all on its own it screws up the text I am working on, but I immediately recognize that it is not really a blameworthy object.

While religion is virtually the inevitable result of our "maturationally natural" cognitions, science does not come naturally. "Nature does not groom human minds for carrying out the *disciplined criticism of theories* that is the obligation of science." Instead, "sciences' radical counterintuitiveness makes it cognitively unnatural in the extreme. . . . Some ideas have natural disadvantages cognitively; science's esoteric interests, radically counterintuitive claims, and specialized forms of thinking are perfect examples. Such ideas are not easy to acquire, nor easy to retain, nor easy to communicate. Acquiring and engaging the cognitive tools necessary to make use of these ideas cuts directly against the grain of our maturationally natural cognitive dispositions." Science relentlessly critiques our natural cognitive proclivities, religions play upon them. However, no real evidence (ethnographic studies for example) is offered that "popular" religion is really as widespread and "popular," that is, simplistically focused on supernatural powers, as this discussion implies.

But there is a deeper difference between religion and science at work here. Religious explanations "focus on agent causality and take a narrative form." On the other hand, science "has, over time, steadily restricted the domains in which appeal to agent causality (of any sort) are any longer deemed legitimate." So "popular" religion's virtually exclusive reliance on our supposed default proclivity to overattribute events to intentional agents, provides an even deeper contrast with science than its uncritical dependence on maturationally natural cognitions.

Science's current preference for impersonal mechanistic models rather than intentional ones is reiterated throughout the text. Despite McCauley's valorization of the "*disciplined criticism of theories*" science's drive for the impersonal is not critically interrogated at all. As for example, it was in Erwin Schrödinger's essay "Mind and Matter," where he argues, correctly in my estimation, that the impersonal view of the world is the inevitable result of science's chosen method since Galileo. It is a methodological commitment, not a complete, ontological description. As such it does not logically rule out other, additional ways of conceiving of the world.

McCauley nuances his dichotomy of religion and science in at least three ways. First, unlike many of the debunkers of religion who totally dichotomize science and religion, McCauley stresses that "*all* of the cognitive differences between science and religion that I explore in this book are differences of degree" (emphasis in original). He insists that "I wish merely to argue for the *comparative* unnaturalness of science," and that not "everything cognitive about religion is rooted in maturationally natural cognitive systems (systematic theologies are not) nor that nothing cognitive about science is."

Second, he shies away from making grandiose claims, such as that his theory has "explained religion." Rather he recognizes that "an analysis of the cognitive naturalness of religion . . . does not provide a comprehensive theory of religious cognition, let alone a comprehensive theory of religion." A point I certainly agree with.

And third, he affirms that there is more to "religion" than simple appeals to agent causation. Religion too has its critical, intellectual dimension, which in many ways parallels science. He writes,

> In the course of refining religious formulations to increase their consistency and coherence, theologians avail themselves of many of the same tools scientists use. Typically theologians are experts at conceptual analysis and at carrying out the same forms of deductive inference that play such a noteworthy role in science . . . some religions are fully capable of provoking (and supporting) extended reflection about the complicated logical, conceptual, explanatory, and empirical issues that religious representations reliably engender. Like science, these conscious, thought-full, theological activities can spawn representations that depart substantially from the deliverances of our maturationally natural cognitive systems.

In these ways he undermines any strict science-versus-religion—especially religion's theological-philosophical aspects—dichotomy. Rather, "in some important respects, such

theological projects are on a par cognitively with science ...
[their] processes of argument and debate that are similar in
many respects to those carried out in other scholarly inquiries,
including scientific ones." The difference between theology and
science is not deeply methodological. Both use reflective cognition. The main difference is that in theology, "appeals to agent
explanation/causality" are "unrestricted," while in science they
are "restricted."

Given McCauley's nuancing of the religion-science distinction, one might be forgiven for wondering how strong the book's
conclusion really is. Even among the most secular populations,
I have often heard expressed a vague "sense" or "intuition" that
there must be a "God" or a "higher power." That such feelings are
common is hard to deny. Likewise, no one denies that learning
mathematical physics, biochemistry, or statistics is hard work. Is
this all the main argument boils down to? And how much interpretative gain really comes from comparing two such disparate
human phenomena? A point we will return to.

So if the science-religion distinction is so nuanced, even
weakened, what is the point? I think readers must wait till the
end to get the book's main thrust: "It is atheism, not religion,
that humans must work to acquire. Compared with atheism, or
science, popular religion ... make(s) comparatively light cognitive demands on human minds." Another subtext: atheists are
hardworking intellectuals; religious folk, except perhaps for
a few theologians, are intellectually lazy, simply following the
cognitive path of least resistance.

While McCauley nuances his account of the relationship
between science and religion and makes it clear he is referring
only to "popular" religion, others have been blunter. We have
already seen Boyer insist simply that religion is "the path of least
resistance for our cognitive system," while "disbelief is generally the result of deliberate, effortful work." E. O Wilson gets to

the heart of the matter when he says bluntly, "the human mind evolved to believe in gods. It did not evolve to believe in biology." Notice that once again we are comparing two very different things: a simple proposition, belief in God, and a very complex social practice, biology. The mind surely did not evolve to believe in biology. But, presumably, it did evolve to believe in causality, to recognize patterns, to distinguish living from nonliving things, and to be curious. That is, it evolved all the specific cognitive pillars of the complex practice of biology. If we applied the same methods to biology that are often applied to religion in this literature, if we simply broke biology down into its component parts and argued that each evolved in a different module for a different purpose that had nothing to do with producing biological theories, but only with surviving in the wilds, then we would have to conclude, would we not, that biology is simply a misfiring or misdirection of our evolved cognitive processes that developed for other purposes? Presumably we all understand that biology is not simply a gathering of relatively disconnected modular cognitive tools that some cultures accidentally joined together as part of their own struggle for survival, but is rather an integrated and complex arena of understanding. Likewise, developed religions are more than simply a "belief in God" or a loose collection of supposedly "modular" cognitive tools.

This contrast is (again!) based mainly on research on children's cognition, which suggests that convictions about supernatural agents, "intuitive dualism," and teleological thinking come naturally to children. Religion is then described as simply the result of these automatic, implicit, childish cognitive structures and the holding of these rather simple beliefs, whereas science is described as the result of hard work and discipline. No one doubts that learning biochemistry or working on problems in mathematical physics takes hard work. But no one who trains in yoga or martial arts as a spiritual practice, or who goes on thirty-day Zen retreats or studies the *Upanishads*, especially in the original Sanskrit, or Nargajuna's *Madhyamaka-karika*, or Aquinas's *Summa*, would recognize that as a description of their religious practice. One might just as well contrast practicing yoga or meditation or reading Nargajuna or Aquinas with a child memorizing the multiplication tables or catching butterflies in the field next door and conclude that religion demands discipline and effort while math and science come naturally to children. McCauley would presumably agree with me here, since he clearly contrasts "popular religion" with "theology," whose intellectuality compares to science. But he may be making gross and unsupported generalizations about "popular" religion. Who really falls under that umbrella term?

So what is "religion" in this argument that religion comes naturally but science demands hard work? It seems that the definition of religion here includes everything that could possibly ever be called religion. What is science in this argument? Science is defined very narrowly. Again, an interesting rhetorical strategy: compare a very, very specific and narrow understanding of science with a very general understanding of religion. Yes, children may naturally believe in God, but not in quarks. But children soon learn to add and subtract, or memorize simple chemical formulas, but do not naturally understand the *Heart Sutra*. Also, such a claim completely dichotomizes religion and science. That is a modern polemic. The history of science reveals centuries of close connections between religion and science, another fact ignored by the debunkers or missed by their schemas.

In order to make this polemical contrast of natural religion and unnatural science work, many of its advocates make two moves. First, they treat both science and religion as sets of beliefs and concepts; and second, they abstract these concepts out of the actual context in which they live and function. Both moves are highly problematic. First, the comparison depends on an overly simplistic, unidimensional view of religion. In few religions is "belief in propositions" the heart of the matter. This highly intellectualistic, disembodied view of religion, and even of belief, is in keeping with the cognitivist frame of reference found in these writings. Religion is seen as another, even if mistaken, example of disembodied representational rationality. This is a projection of cognitivism onto religion. Again, the complexity of the life of religion is lost in this abstraction of a few concepts like gods and souls, which are then made to stand for the whole phenomenon. You can study the basic structures of a cell, such as membranes, proteins, etc. This is very important work. But it would be ridiculous to claim on that basis alone, that you have "explained" all of biology. You have explained a tiny fraction of the whole field but you have not touched on how cells combine, how organisms form, and what functions biological knowledge might serve. You have not "explained biology."

Likewise, helping us understand some of the cognitive processes at work when a person says they believe in a concept called "God" and "the soul" can be very interesting. But do not claim you have thereby "explained religion." You have said nothing about how such concepts might relate to others in religious discourse. You have said nothing about how these concepts function in the life of the believer. You have missed the transforming impact of practices whose "meaning" is not primarily referential, but rather transformational—"by their fruits you will know them"—as well as any possible forms of knowing that are not primarily sense-data driven or outwardly focused. This move distorts both religion and science; for religion and science are both networks of practices whose concepts make little sense apart from those practices. Unlike some other cognitive scientists, in relation to religion, McCauley appears to agree, for he says directly that his cognitive model is not an explanation of religion in general.

Second, this abstract definition of religion and science as sets of beliefs is then further abstracted out of the lived experience of science and religion. Science, especially as discussed by the debunkers, is always an elite practice by a cohort of highly trained and disciplined experts. When they mention science, they do not have in mind fifth graders touring the Museum of Natural History. They have in mind mathematical physicists and biochemists. Obviously, understanding super-string theory, which only a handful of people in the world can do, or the symmetries of elementary particles or the physiology of the immune system takes great discipline and hard work. Only a few can do it. Doing that kind of science is an elite activity. The debunkers are right.

As McCauley himself emphasizes throughout his book, religion, as he means the term, is not an elite activity; religion is potentially a practice for all men and women. A congregation I was recently associated with contained many elite scientists. The presence of several universities and medical research facilities in New Jersey guaranteed that. There were also many working in computer science and information technology—the presence of many of those institutes and research centers guaranteed that—as well as business people, and laborers and skilled tradesmen and women. The type of language that speaks to that range of humanity is obviously going to be very different from the language used by a tightly disciplined professional cohort. To compare the professional language of working scientists to a discourse designed to speak to the experiences of astrophysicists and plumbing contractors together seems rather illogical. And are these trained professionals who are also religious practitioners examples of "popular" religion? They are not theologians, but that hardly means their religion is totally uncritical and unreflective.

It is a particularly vicious rhetorical move when these two different languages are compared and evaluated by the criteria of only one of them, that of elite science. Religious language is demeaned in this comparison. Boyer calls religious language "an airy nothing," and Dennett writes that religious beliefs are "incomprehensible," "downright unintelligible," and display "sheer incoherence." All this because they fall short of the formal precision of physics and biochemistry. We do not demean the language of biochemistry if it fails to provide us moral guidance or evoke in us a spirit of worship and devotion, or catalyze personal transformations. This is a crucial theme that we will return to again and again, especially in chapter 5. This comparison of religion as simple beliefs flowing from children's natural cognitions with the advanced theories of natural science assumes that such concepts are, in some sense, comparable. Not only are their lived contexts radically different, an elite professional group versus potentially all of humanity, but their functions are radically different as well. Only if one can demonstrate that science and religion perform the same functions in practice can one justifiably compare them. I will suggest in the last chapter that is far from the case. All I want to say here is that such a case must be made if this comparison is to be justified.

Comparing complex reasoning either in science or religion with the simple beliefs and activities of children is an invidious comparison whichever way it goes. But it is a very effective rhetorical strategy. If I want to pick a fight or mount a crusade or confuse an issue, misleading comparisons, oversimplifications, emotionally charged language, and dichotomous black-and-white thinking are the strategies to use. I have heard them over and over from many pulpits in many religious congregations. But if I want understanding, more complex cognitive strategies are necessary.

Truth Claims

Besides being a rhetorical strategy, this sliding quickly from the findings of cognitive research to implying that religion is everywhere mistaken is a confused move. From cognitive science we learn that religious ideas and behaviors are human artifacts, utilizing human cognitive systems. And they are constrained and shaped by these systems. The same is no doubt true of economics, physics, and cognitive science. But we do not usually say that tells us anything about the truth of the claims found in those domains. As I argued previously, it is a serious, logical error to say that understanding the psychological drivers of a claim implies anything about the truth of the claim. A person who studies the motivations that propel a person to be an economist and the cognitions employed there would be, to paraphrase a statement I heard from Justin Barrett, flabbergasted if someone said his research answered the question of whether the law of supply and demand holds true in a globalized economy. A person who studies the motivations that propel a person to be a physicist and the cognitions employed there would be flabbergasted if someone said his research answered the question of whether string theory is correct. Somehow religion is different. The debunkers say that learning about the motivations that propel a person's religious practices and the cognitions employed there implies that religion false. The whole point of the cognitive science of religion is that religion is no different cognitively from other human activities. Yet when it comes to religion's claims, it is treated differently. There's a double standard, but no justification is given for that double standard.

For the debunkers that double standard requires no justification. For them religion is different. It is a criminal act. It is a disease. That's how it appears against a backdrop of the conviction that science is the only arbiter of reality and truth. Like all implicit processing, the intuitive cognitions that drive this background conviction do not have to be conscious, do not have to be explicated, do not have to be defended. But like all intuitions, they can be made conscious and evaluated.

I have suggested that the crusaders' rhetorical use of the findings of cognitive science to debunk religion appears compelling against a background in which science is the only arbiter of reality and truth; a context in which science is the only valid way to understand the world. What is that claim? Is it an assumption necessary to the conduct of science? Clearly not. Many who have done unquestionably brilliant scientific work in a variety of fields have not shared it. Is it a conclusion based on evidence? Clearly not. No conceivable experiment could prove it true or false. It is simply not falsifiable. So what is it? It is an article of faith. It is a creed. Presumably it is found compelling by some people because of the operation of the same tacit, perhaps unconscious, cognitive processes that are at work in our judgments about any worldview or frame of reference.

While no coercive proofs or unquestionable evidences can be offered to compel agreement in the domain of intuitive cognitions and background assumptions, they can still be made more conscious and critically examined. To the task of critically examining what seems to me to be the background assumptions and tacit sensibilities in which the debunkers' interpretations of cognitive science are deployed we now turn.

Chapter 3

Physicalism

Is a Purely Physicalist Account Compelling?

As with all rational activity in all disciplines, the debunkers arguments are formulated against a set of background assumptions and judgments that make the antireligion crusaders' interpretations of cognitive science compelling to them. In this chapter I will suggest that this background has three components: (1) a reductive physicalist view of reality; (2) a positivistic outlook that claims natural science as the only path to knowledge; and (3) an understanding of human culture modeled on Darwinian evolutionary theory. I will argue here that none of these positions is as rational or compelling as the debunkers of religion wish it to be.

Reductive Physicalism

Both positions, a religious outlook and a narrowly physicalist one, depend on background assumptions that may rest on more basic intuitive sensibilities about reality. The previous chapter emphasized that such background assumptions cannot be proven in a formal sense, since they form the axioms on the basis of which any proof would be constructed. That is, I do not prove the axioms of Euclidian geometry. I choose to "accept" them or "commit myself" to them. Only having done that, can I then use them to construct the proofs that characterize Euclidian geometry. I can construct a model of Euclidian space from which I can then derive the axioms of Euclidian geometry. But the construction of such a model will have its own, deeper axioms and so this only pushes the problem back a step. In every discipline, I do not prove the basic axioms, for they are the basis of any proof I construct. This means that there is no way to prove the truth of physicalism to the person who does not accept physicalist assumptions or to prove the truth of a religious outlook to someone who does accept physicalist assumptions. Even though basic assumptions cannot be proven, reasons can still be given for them. And reasonable discussion can take place between people with different basic assumptions. But the reasons given will not be coercive proofs. Reason cannot ultimately decide between two sets of basic convictions. Their claims to our assent rest on other grounds.

Many recent, rather polemical writings by the so-called New Atheists, many of whom draw on the interpretations of cognitive science discussed previously, appear to simply assume that physicalism or something close to it is the default rational position. Therefore, if they can demonstrate the falsity of any and all claims about a knowable reality beyond the world as described by empirical science, the default position will automatically be some form of physicalism. This assumption that there are only two possibilities is itself worth further analysis, and we will get to that in time. My purpose now is only to challenge the assumption that physicalism, in the very restricted way I have defined it (that is, the way the debunkers and others rely on it), should be regarded as the default rational position. My aim is to show that there are serious, I think fatal, problems with this reductive physicalism as the fundamental view of reality. There is not space to develop any of them in depth. Each deserves a book or books to do that properly. My point is only to argue that there are good reasons not to simply assume or accept uncritically a narrow physicalist model of the world. Obviously, given what I said above, showing that such reductive physicalism may not be rationally tenable in no way demonstrates that any religious outlook necessarily is. It is only to show that the kind of physicalism that seems to be the basis on which so many current antireligious polemics, especially those relying on cognitive science, depend may not be as compelling as the authors hope. In chapter 4 we will discuss the possibility of more complex versions of physicalism than the ones that many of the debunkers of religion appear to rely on. This chapter focuses on problems with the more narrow forms of physicalism that seem necessary to support the antireligious polemics of the cognitive scientists discussed earlier.

Is Such Physicalism Compelling?

There follow nine problems with a purely physicalist understanding of the world. They are basically just listed to make the point that physicalism is not as automatically compelling as the debunkers wish. Many questions can be raised about them and each of these would require a book or more to develop in depth.

(1) Of course the most basic problem with a physicalist position is that the claim that the only reality is physical reality, as demonstrated by the physical sciences, is a claim that is itself not demonstrable by the physical sciences. No conceivable experiment could demonstrate that. Nor is it a regulative principle of some kind that science itself requires. Throughout history there have been brilliant scientists doing excellent work who do not

accept it. Accepting such a claim is not required for the conduct of science, nor is it demonstrable scientifically. So the "prestige" of science cannot be called on as proof for physicalist metaphysics. So what is such a claim? It is a matter of belief, of commitment, of judgment. It has exactly the same logical status as the contrary claim that the physical world as investigated by science is not the entirety of all that is real and that empirical science is not the only source of knowledge.

(2) In addition to this logical problem, the claim that only physical things exist is clearly not a physical thing, at least in our ordinary sense. It is an idea. Now some physicalists want to claim that mental realities are really physical realities. But that claim is hardly straightforward or uncontested. Finally, the only defense for it is that since thoughts clearly are real and since only physical things are real, thoughts must be in some sense entirely physical. But, of course, such an argument is virtually a tautology and tautologies can tell us nothing about reality since they simply reprise their premises in different words and can be true under any and all conditions. The claim that all unmarried men are bachelors, on the premise that bachelor means unmarried man, is true by definition. It would be true whether unmarried men existed or not. Likewise the claim that thoughts are both real and entirely physical, on the premise that real means entirely physical, is true whether or not such things as entirely physical thoughts exist. This is not a demonstration of the truth of the claim, but once again a confusion of premise and conclusion. Of course, not all those who call themselves physicalists reject the reality of mental phenomena. We will discuss them in the next chapter. Those I am referring to here, the narrowly reductive physicalists, tend to, or hope to, eliminate mental contents from the set of what is real.

(3) This general problem of specifying the reality of "mental" contents is even sharper in the domain of science than in

ordinary life. Modern science depends on mathematical objects and logical truths. But mathematical and logical objects are clearly primarily mental. They are clearly not physical objects perceived by our five senses. Thus their status has been the subject of philosophical debate for centuries. There is no need to review that discussion here. But the position that only physical things, things available to the five senses and describable in physical terms, exist raises serious questions about the reality of the mathematical forms on which science depends. Thus one wonders if a purely physicalist position can sustain an understanding of the scientific method that is necessary for the conduct of science.

(4) In addition, it is hard to say what "physical" means in the light of contemporary physics. Electrons are probability waves, appearing as "particles" only when measured in a specific way. Fixed meanings for matter, time, and space are almost impossible to specify. Mathematical formalisms suggest that "matter" is vibrations of "waves," but waves that lack any physical medium; think of ocean waves with no ocean. According to some, like Stephen Hawking, "imaginary time" is the real time. What we experience as time is a function of the limitations of human consciousness that only perceives four (time and three dimensions of Euclidean space) of the many actual dimensions. So it is, likewise, with "space," which is so bound up with matter and time that their lack of specifiablity carries over to it. Thus a physicalism that insists that "matter," in the sense of that which exists in Euclidean space and ruthlessly obeys Newton's laws, is the foundational reality to which everything must be referred, and in terms of which everything must be understood, has very little claim today to the title of science.

A corollary of this is that what we do know of the physical world through physics is only a segment of that reality, as it appears under very artificially isolated and constrained experimental conditions. The physical world we know is only the physical world as it appears to human consciousness within a restricted framework. There is absolutely no reason to claim that this is the entire picture.

(5) Consciousness remains inexplicable in strictly physicalist terms. Despite physicalists' breathtakingly extravagant and breezy claims that science has demonstrated that mind/consciousness is but the product of brain activity, nothing could be further from the truth. Assertions of this claim are not reports of experimental findings, but are simply a report of physicalist ideology. We cannot even specify what a physical account of consciousness might look like. Physicalists may well hope, in the theological sense of the "conviction of things not seen," as the New Testament says, that in the future such an explanation may be forthcoming. But it should be called for what it is, an act of faith. A corollary is that the interrelated issues of "mental causation," freedom, and intentionality, like conscious awareness too, continue to escape a compelling physicalist explanation. Some physicalists tacitly acknowledge this and end up arguing that consciousness, freedom and intentionality are illusions or epiphenomena. Such a move has a long history in the scientific world. If you don't like something that doesn't fit within your theory, just deny its reality. When J. J. Thomson proposed the idea of subatomic particles, his colleagues thought he was playing a joke. All this will be discussed in more depth in the next chapter.

(6) Accounting for morality and values remains problematic. Evolutionary psychology may provide an account of the evolutionary functions of our moral sensitivities and conscience. But no one has found any logical way to derive the actual content of our values from empirical investigations of the physical world. They tell us what is the case in the physical world. However, empirical descriptions of what "is" tell us very little about what "ought to be."

(7) There remains the irony that research suggests that human flourishing requires a sense of meaning and purpose. People who experience life as meaningful, who have values by which they live, who possess a grounded hopefulness, appear to do better on almost every epidemiological measure and to be more resilient and better able to cope. If meaning, purpose, value, hope, and other such metaphysical variables are really, objectively meaningless as they are on purely physicalist terms (e.g., physicist Steven Weinberg's famous claim that the more we understand the universe, the more meaningless it appears), then we have evolved into a major psychological and spiritual "double bind" and psychologists know that double binds make human beings crazy. Some physicalists do embrace this double bind and argue that evolution has produced an objectively determined, meaningless species (us), endowed with the illusion that it possesses freedom and intentionality and purpose because such illusions have survival value. Slingerland writes, "we are robots designed not to believe that we are robots." How would we possibility know whether such a perplexing assertion was true or false? How could such a confused proposition compel our rational assent?

(8) Science itself assumes a rational structure to the world. On purely physicalist terms, there is no reason to think that such a rational, intelligible structure actually exists. Physicalism seeks to understand the world in the most rational way possible, but is unable to give any rational account for the rationality it requires. As Nietzsche pointed out, truth itself functions as a value. But if the truth is that all values are meaningless, then truth too is meaningless. Even if it possess the strictest possible methodology, which evolutionary psychology, cognitive psychological studies of cultural phenomena, and physicalist philosophy certainly do not, it is hard to call a paradigm scientific that undercuts grounds for believing in the reality of reason and

truth. In addition, as Hume pointed out, on physicalist terms which limit "reality" to objects known through the physical senses, inductive reasoning and claims about causation cannot be substantiated. Simple sensory experience of events occurring in conjunction is not a sufficient basis for inferring an occult force known as causality. A position that undermines the bases of scientific work, such as causality, rationality and truth in the name of science seems a bit self-contradictory.

(9) The age-old question of a final explanation of the universe is not answered, but is rather ruled out of court. Likewise with questions about why anything exists rather than utter nothingness; or why what exists contains the potential to form into a universe or universes that contains or contain the further potential to give rise to and to sustain sentient life. Physicalism insists that such final explanations are necessarily impossible. But that does not automatically make them irrational. There is no evidence that it is psychopathological to wonder about such things. Such questions are impossible only in a purely physicalist context. Religious worldviews can provide additional resources and perspectives with which to reflect on such questions.

These nine concerns, and more could be listed, suggest that the assumption that reductive physicalism and the interpretations derived from it are the viewpoints that are most comprehensive, most rationally compelling, and most congruent with science may not be correct. All these problems do not coercively prove such physicalism wrong; nor do they demonstrate that alternative viewpoints are necessarily correct. And I have already argued that such fundamental viewpoints are not subject to coercive proof or demonstration, since they are the basis on which and the context in which proofs and demonstrations are constructed. Instead, my only point is that some popular science writers and polemical atheists are wrong to simply assume or assert, without giving any reasons, that science requires belief in physicalism (i.e., the belief that the physical world as described by natural science is the only objective reality). Or to claim that physicalism is obviously the most convincing, comprehensive, and rational viewpoint. It appears that a very narrow form of physicalism is the background that sustains the debunkers' antireligious interpretations of cognitive science. If that background is not so obviously or intuitively plausible, than neither is the antireligious interpretation of cognitive science.

Positivism: How to Misunderstand Rationality

The debunking interpretations of cognitive science are often based on a positivist model of human rationality in which there are simple facts and stark dichotomies between objectivity and subjectivity, belief and fact, reason and irrationality, and in which scientific verification as they understand it is the only guide to truth. Scott Atran even quotes A. J. Ayer, whose 1950s' philosophy of "Logical Positivism" clearly articulated this position, which then was rejected by virtually every philosopher of science before the end of the twentieth century. Ayer relentlessly insisted that only statements that directly described sense experience are meaningful and only claims verifiable by laboratory experiments are truthful. Moral statements were simply accounts of feelings. Metaphysical and religious concepts were strictly meaningless. Meaningful statements referred directly to the immediate data of the senses. All else was nonsense.

Dennett's *Breaking the Spell* seems to embrace the same, outmoded Positivism when he writes, "canonical religious beliefs cannot be tested for truth"; "[they] are not subject to (scientific, historical) confirmation"; they are "beyond observation, beyond meaningful test." He grandly asserts that "there is no better source of truth on any topic than well conducted science." [Dan, do you really mean that? Do you really feel that the most important truths about attending a concert are found by calculating sinusoidal wave frequencies? Or that the most important truths about conjugal relations are revealed by psychophysiological measures taken during the "act"? Really?!] The Positivists' assertion that the only meaningful process of verification is scientific verification runs headlong into a host of problems, not the least of which is that the claim itself is impossible to verify scientifically. And the idea that there is a single method of verification, even in the natural sciences, is heavily contested and rarely affirmed.

The debunkers appear to feel there is no alternative to Positivism except the complete relativism of an extreme version of "postmodernism" (see, for example, the appendix "Science" in Dennett's *Breaking the Spell* or Slingerland's *What Science Offers the Humanities*). But surely we can count past "one" or at most "two" when it comes to ways of rationally understanding the world. Here is an example again from my own field. Why does a person fall ill with depression or high blood pressure? Is there a single answer to that? Is there only one way to go about answering that question? Clearly not. There are genetic predispositions, uncovered by a combination of laboratory research and epidemiological studies. There are psychodynamic processes arising from childhood experience (abuse, parental neglect, attachment relationships) uncovered through careful clinical interviews. There are environmental factors (pollution, poverty, conflicts at work and at home) uncovered by sociological surveys and qualitative analysis. There are behavioral, life-style dimensions and the patient's current thoughts, feelings, and moods revealed by intake screening procedures. There are neurophysiological factors assessed by blood tests and the effects of medication. And, while not directly contributing to the treatment of a particular patient, there is a great deal of theoretical work done by philosophers of medicine and other theoreticians to provide the categories necessary for interpreting all these findings. All of these contribute to answering the question of why a person becomes ill. All of them are clearly rational, but they all depend on different types of rationality, different methodologies, and different theoretical models. Fleeing a radical postmodern relativism does not require insistence on a single method (empiricism narrowly defined), on a single interpretive approach (physicalism), or on a single acceptable outcome (physicalist explanations). There is more than one rational possibility.

Note here that Dennett and his colleagues are doing two things simultaneously that need to be thought of separately. First, they are reporting on findings from the cognitive science of religion. This is scientific work and should be evaluated by the evidence presented and the coherence of the theories which are offered. In the first chapter I tried to survey that work as fairly as possible and to affirm the importance of that project. This research describes possible motivations, mechanisms, and processes and says absolutely nothing about the truth or falsity of any claims about any transcendental realities. I see no problems in general with such investigations.

Second, they are using cognitive science to try to breathe new life into an outdated positivist project. When Dennett says things like "religious beliefs cannot be tested for truth . . . [they] are not subject to (scientific, historical) confirmation . . . [and are] beyond observation, beyond meaningful test"; when Boyer calls religion an "airy nothing"; when Atran quotes A. J. Ayer and writes that religious claims are not "truth-valuable . . . liable to verification, falsification, or logical evaluation," they are standing in that positivist lineage, even if they were to reject the label of Logical Positivism. By "meaningful test" and not liable to "verification, falsification, or logical evaluation," they clearly mean "scientific testing and verification." So all this really boils down to the assertion that religion is not science. An assertion almost all religious persons today would agree with. Hardly a radical claim. It bites only if it is conjoined with the assertions that science alone is the only means of arriving at knowledge and that scientific verification is the only legitimate kind of verification. That assumption is the core of the positivist project which the current debunkers of religion are attempting to resurrect under the banner of cognitive science. But this is not an empirical issue. This is a philosophical project that most philosophers of science today think outdated. The idea that only scientific language is meaningful, rational, and "truth-valuable" is very hard to defend under any conditions. It is only remotely defensible under the condition of a reductive, physicalist worldview. And obviously one of the tasks of this book is to awaken some skepticism about such a worldview as the only compelling and valid one.

The Cartesian wish at the dawn of the age of science was that disciplined rationality, doubting everything, limiting claims to direct observations, and following the dictates of linear logic, would remove any traces of the personal and arrive at totally impersonal, objective, and therefore certain knowledge. The problem is that there are no raw data, no impersonal observations, and no direct, unmediated data reports. Disciplined, trained observers experience things within a framework, precisely because they are trained and disciplined. One has to be specially trained to observe things in a certain way, whether in science or religion, and to draw certain specified conclusions. The point is not that all claims are equally compelling—that is obviously false—but rather that all compelling claims are shaped by contextual and personal factors that make them compelling. Similar factors made other claims compelling in the past that we now, because of analogous factors, no longer find compelling. The fact-theory dichotomy that insists there are "naked" facts directly perceived, which is at the heart of a positivist outlook, has clearly been shown to be untenable. We know something qualifies as a "fact" only because we encounter it in the context of a theory that tells us what a fact is. We need theory to tell us what is a fact and what isn't, what are good data, bad data, and not data at all. So the positivists' picture of understanding as simply directly comparing claims and with some clear, neutral data is a nice wish. But human understanding, even in science, simply does not work that way. As my late friend Ian Barbour often said, "the facts always come theory-laden."

This inability to directly compare our claims with some simple facts, which is the heart of the debunkers' positivism, is because of what philosophers of science refer to by the technical phrase "the underdetermination of theory by data." This basically says that there can be many theories (some argue for an infinite number) that are logically consistent with any set of facts. One example is the rash of college suicides discussed earlier, when several different, empirically supported theories were offered. One of the philosophers who emphasized this was W. V. O. Quine, who was a strict empiricist. He acknowledged this problem when he wrote, "I do, qua lay physicist, believe in physical objects and not in Homer's gods; and I consider it a scientific error to believe otherwise. But in point of epistemological footage the physical objects and the gods differ only in degree and not in kind." And McCauley insists that the cognitive differences between science and religion, especially in its reflective, theological form, are differences of degree. Thus science cannot claim the kind of epistemologically privileged *carte blanche* that the debunkers often seek to give it.

This hard and fast reason versus irrationality dichotomy so often employed by the antireligious crusaders, presupposes a unitary understanding of rationality that is profoundly unconvincing. The rationality needed to solve a problem in classical mechanics is rather different from the rationality needed to diagnose a disease in a patient, and that is very different from the rationality used to decide if a person is guilty beyond a "reasonable" doubt. But they are all considered rational. Likewise, it is hard to maintain that Nargajuna's treatise *Madhyamika-karika* or Aquinas's *Summa Theologiae* are not "reasoned." This rather suggests that it can be rational to call for different types of reasoning in different domains. And specific arguments would have to be given to show why the reasoning of a Nargajuna or an Aquinas or that found in the *Upanishads* should be excluded from a necessarily more pluralistic definition of rationality. McCauley suggests something similar when he compares positively the intellectual work of religious reflection with that of the sciences. In keeping with their love of pathological metaphors (a form of discourse I personally don't much like, even though I am a clinical person), we might say that the debunkers are suffering from a rational stenosis, a constriction.

How to Forget to Look in the Mirror

Cognitive scientific explanations are presumably compelling for cognitive scientific reasons. They too are the outcome of human, cognitive activity. That does not disqualify them automatically. So it is not clear why that should automatically disqualify religious accounts. For me, the most frustrating thing about the accounts based on cognitive science offered by the crusaders against religion is their amazing lack of reflexivity. Dennett is a partial exception here, as is McCauley. Most of these authors do not mention the fact that their claims are presumably also the expression of innate cognitive mechanisms, that whatever limitations that might present to religion also apply to their theories. Any implications that might flow from an analysis of science or cognitive science using the categories of cognitive science itself are rarely discussed here. Slingerland does note in reference to science that "The thought processes involved in reaching such counterintuitive conclusions [as those found in physics] are merely extensions of thought habits that are *themselves* quite intuitive" (emphasis in original). Very much like religion. Again, McCauley makes the same point. But if that fact debunks or undermines religion, it must also debunk or undermine science. Again, there is a double standard with no justification given. Or if that fact imposes limits on religious claims, the same cognitively derived limits should apply to the claims of natural and cognitive science. But little such reflexivity can be found in the writings of many of these cognitive scientists.

It is beyond the scope of this book to conduct a whole cognitive science study of cognitive science itself, except to point out the obvious places where the same processes that are implicated in religious ideas—the role of schemas, the distinction between implicit and explicit domains, the shaping of conscious rationality by tacit, unconscious processes—are also at work in cognitive science. And whatever limitations this might impose on religious ideas are also imposed on the ideas of cognitive science itself.

This refusal to apply to one's own scientific theories the analysis one applies to others, which often seems endemic in cognitive science, reflects a cultural context in which science is the one cultural domain that is not taught with reference to its social and historical location; unless one accidentally happens on a course in the history or sociology of science, and even there the history of science can be taught from a simple self-aggrandizing position as the continual triumph of truth over ignorance. The fact that science too is a human, cultural project, subject to the same limitations and constraints as all other human, cultural projects, rarely enters into these discussions.

The response often given is that science transcends culture since its findings are true regardless of culture. Everywhere in the world, falling objects obey Newton's law and polio is caused by a virus. But that is to confuse scientific process with scientific findings. The objects found by fundamental physics or molecular biology may, in some sense, exist in the world independent of culture. But the terms in which they are categorized and the process that led to their discovery, reflect a human process that drew on and was constrained by the categories available in a specific culture at a specific time. For example, some discoveries in mechanics could not have been made before calculus was invented. Likewise, some cosmological theories require multidimensional geometries. Or I told the tale of the resistance to "mind-body" medicine, because an overly mechanistic ethos pervaded twentieth-century medicine. Likewise, such things as meteor craters or subatomic particles were resisted at first because the prevailing cultural framework could not accommodate them. The findings of science, although not the categories in which they are described, may in some sense stand a bit outside of culture. But the process that is science is always embedded in a culture. And disciplinary self-knowledge requires that we reflect on the ways we might be culturally constrained when we propose, among other things, cognitive explanations for religion. Ironically though, while physicalists seem to want to account for other fields, like religion, solely by physicalist explanations, they want their own work to be understood more humanistically, as the result of rational choices, personal discipline, and not simply as the result of deterministic forces. They want their own work to be appreciated as a uniquely human, cultural achievement.

Another example of this apparent lack of self-awareness can be seen in the lack of acknowledgment of the limits of functional explanations, especially their inability to decide the truth of claims. Justin Barrett is an exception here. Psychologists routinely acknowledge that their accounts of a phenomenon deal only with the psychological cause or function of that phenomenon. But clearly claims we regard as true and claims we regard as false can both have similar psychological causes. They arise out of a person's life history or their tacit cognitions and fulfill similar psychological functions, such as relief of anxiety, satisfying curiosity, creating social solidarity, etc. For example, Bloom writes correctly that "we see purpose, intention, design even when it is not there." Of course, but we also see them when they are there, in the intentional actions of our friends and families, in the workings of the well-designed cars we drive and the computers we write with. Unless Bloom is claiming that all purpose, intention, and design are everywhere illusory. But that is a vast metaphysical claim that cognitive science, even at its most grandiose, is incapable of demonstrating. How do we know when this perceptual mistake is happening and when it is not? Presumably something other than cognitive science is required to answer that. But in the case of religion, some cognitive scientists seem to feel that cognitive science itself, grounded in a reductive physicalism, is all that is needed to assure us that mistake is always happening. Again, rather than self-critically exploring its own limitations, especially when it investigates religion, cognitive science appears to grant itself an exception to those limits.

What Is a Scientific Study of Religion?

Dennett's book *Breaking the Spell* is an extended argument that science should study religion. Obviously that is a project I am totally in agreement with. I am a long-time member of something called the Society for the Scientific Study of Religion. Some years ago I was elected a fellow of a division of the American Psychological Association titled the "Psychology of Religion." I served for six years as the vice-president of the International Association for the Psychology of Religion. Studying religion scientifically has been a major pillar of my professional life. What perplexes me about Dennett's book is clearly not that appeal, but rather his tacit sense that this is a new enterprise that he must fearlessly advocate rather than something that has been going on for generations. The Society for the Scientific Study of Religion was founded right after the Second World War and the precursor to the current International Association goes back to the nineteenth century in Europe. For generations, members of these and other scientific bodies have been studying religion with qualitative and quantitative methods widely regarded as scientific. Yet Dennett writes as though he is standing up for something new and dangerous.

Beyond that, he alludes to researchers prior to himself and his cohort only in order to demean and dismiss them as doing the equivalent of "bird-watching." Previous work, universally considered scientific in peer-reviewed journals and conference presentations, is now derided as "theoretically innocent," by which I think he means theoretically naïve. Only now are he and his colleagues "beginning, for the first time really, to study the natural phenomenon of religion through the eyes of contemporary science." The current scene, before the advent of Dennett and colleagues, is dismissed as one of "dubious results" being produced by "second-rate" researchers. No "standing on the shoulders of giants" for these brave explorers. The phrase is attributed to Sir Isaac Newton.

What is going on here? After trashing previous scientific studies of religion, Dennett turns immediately to mention

Darwin, implying that the scientific investigation of human behavior and culture is next to worthless without invoking him. So we have here a further narrowing of the epistemological vision. First, all proper understanding is restricted to empirical science, and now even scientific knowledge in the study of the human domain is further restricted to only a Darwinian paradigm. Let us not forget, here Darwinism has been lifted out of its original scientific domain, the biology of speciation, and deployed elsewhere as the only lens through which to view cultural activities like religion. Had the debunkers said that they are analyzing religion using only the methods of a new science still in its infancy (cognitive science) interpreted only by theories removed from their primary scientific context (biological speciation), I would have no objection, since that is, in reality, what they are doing. But that would not generate magazine covers, media interviews, lecture tours, and bestselling books. Better to proclaim that you are "explaining religion" and "breaking the spell."

In keeping with the drive to trash the work of everyone other than your friends—not the attitude I must say that I have found in most scientists I have studied and worked with, even in very contentious areas—Dennett describes, in *Breaking the Spell*, theology as "intellectual tennis without a net" because "an appeal to faith is out of bounds, quite literally, in the serious game of empirical research.... Let's play real intellectual tennis ... with the net of reason always up." No theologians and few, if any scientists I know, think of theology or science as zero-sum games, like tennis, where one side wins and everyone else loses. How about thinking of them and the relations between them, as a dialogue, or a combined search for the truth, or a common task of bettering humanity, or a discussion aimed at mutual understanding? But no. For the debunkers of religion, the science-religion encounter is like the final match at Wimbledon, where one party must decisively defeat the other. I do wonder if that is the best way to arrive at the truth about complex matters.

For Dennett, a very constricted model of scientific research is the only game in town. When he says, "let us play serious intellectual tennis with the net of reason up," what he means by the net of reason is a very narrow and highly contested, even within science, version of the scientific project. I think McCauley would agree with my point since he writes in his book on religion being natural,

> In the course of refining religious formulations to increase their consistency and coherence, theologians avail themselves of many of the same tools scientists use. Typically theologians are experts at conceptual analysis and at carrying out the same forms of deductive inference that play such a noteworthy role in science . . . some religions are fully capable of provoking (and supporting) extended reflection about the complicated logical, conceptual, explanatory, and empirical issues that religious representations reliably engender. Like science, these conscious, thought-full, theological activities can spawn representations that depart substantially from the deliverances of our maturationally natural cognitive systems.

On the other hand, Dennett's offer of a friendly game of tennis is a bit like showing up at the court and having him hand you a golf club and telling you to go to the back court and return his first serve. Better the religious person should tell him to go to the golf course with his new tennis racket and take his first tee shot. The scientist in the laboratory and the theologian in the study are playing different games, with different rules. But that does not logically entail that theology has no rules or boundaries, only that they are different from those of natural science.

Stephen Toulmin, one of the twentieth-century's preeminent philosophers of science, makes this point, which I argue throughout this book, more clearly than I could when he writes,

> Of course "theological" arguments and "religious" questions and answers ... are on a quite different footing, as a matter of logic from scientific and ethical arguments, questions, and answers.... Provided that we remember that religion has other functions than competing with science and ethics on their own grounds, we shall understand that to reject all religious statements for this reason is to make a serious logical blunder ... this is not to say that there is no "reasoning" to be done in theology and religion—it would be highly paradoxical to declare that the writings of Augustine and Aquinas (for example) were not "reasoned." It is only to mark the difference between the kinds of "reasoning" one can sensibly call for in science and ethics, on the one hand, and in religion, on the other.

This is a point the debunkers consistently appear to misunderstand. But, of course, they do understand this. Their culpable misunderstanding is in the service of a deeper and more culpable misunderstanding that a narrowly defined empirical science is the only serious game worth playing. That's how they feel. Fine. But let us recognize that it is only on a court whose entrance sign reads "methodologically restricted empirical science is the only game allowed here" that Dennett's dismissive description of theology makes any sense. Again, no defense of theology is offered here. My only goal is pointing to places where the debunkers' volleys land way wide of the mark.

The idea that there are interesting and important questions other than those currently being investigated by natural science seems incomprehensible to these reductive physicalists.

Such an idea appears to me to be beyond their ken. And that there may be other methods for investigating human experience that still produce useful knowledge other than that supposedly derived from a Darwinian perspective seems to be heretical in their eyes. Of course, there is a context for this. Culturally, increasingly we see the only goal of knowledge as further controlling nature and producing immediate applications for the production of consumer goods. Other goals or values are increasingly neglected and disparaged. The sole measure of knowledge is a narrow, concrete positivistic view of science. Any definition of "explaining" or "understanding" must fit within that framework. Mechanistic science becomes the only way to truly understand the world.

Let me try to be clear. I completely support the idea that science should study religion as vigorously as possible. No harm, in my eyes, can come from that. And more than once in my career have I too been called on to justify the psychological study of religion in the face of these who have thought it sacrilegious. None of this is news to me or many of my colleagues. But I strongly insist, in opposition to the debunkers, that the appropriate scientific goal is understanding religion, not refuting it; or proselytizing for it. Launching crusades is not a scientific endeavor. Scientific research into the motivations and cognitions implicated in religion can, by itself, say nothing about the truth or falsity of religious claims. To attempt to do so is to extend the argument far beyond the data.

The incompleteness of any single frame of reference should serve to mitigate any methodological or theoretical hubris in the scientific study of religion. Methodological tunnel vision almost always leads to epistemological stenosis. In the debunkers' cognitive science of religion, situational variables, correlations between personality types and behaviors, psychophysiological measures, and developmental histories—the heart of scientific research in personality, social, developmental, and clinical psychology—are all swept aside in favor a single appeal to hypothetical, natural mental mechanisms. Rather than seeing cognition as one piece in a much larger puzzle, all other pieces are thrown away and the modular computational model is proclaimed the single key to the only true understanding of religion. We must wonder about this drive to insist on a single explanation.

The debunkers seem to have lost the ability to count past "one." There is only one truth and only one method for arriving at it. Likewise, there can be only one set of influences or causes (physicalist ones) functioning in the world and in the generation of religious ideas. If they can demonstrate that these factors are at work in the rise of religious ideas, then there is no need to look any further. No other possible influences can also be present. Of course, reductive physicalism demands that response. But given the possible limitations of a narrowly physicalist framework, other cultural and even spiritual factors are not necessarily or logically precluded, except as the projection of the physicalist viewpoint.

The Uses and Misuses of Evolutionary Theory

I suggested in the first chapter that strict, laboratory research on the cognitive mechanisms implicated in religious belief and practice cannot by itself explain the origin of religion. They primarily provide accounts of the functioning of cognitive structures but say little about the origin of those structures that supposedly give rise to religion. To "explain" religion, these findings must be linked to evolutionary theory, which claims to uncover the naturalistic sources of those cognitive mechanisms.

Evolutionary theory in conjunction with religion is such a contested area that I hesitate to enter it. So let me try to state clearly that I am not criticizing the "theory of evolution," whatever that generic phrase might refer to. I do not read any sacred text as though it were a textbook on theories of speciation. I do not doubt that species are interconnected and arose from previous species. What I am raising questions about is the attempt to tightly link evolutionary theory and cognitive psychology and then using evolutionary theory to completely account for cultural activities like religion. I do not doubt the use of something called evolutionary theory to explain the origin of the species; but I do wonder how far it can go in explaining the origin of culture and religion.

Current neo-Darwinian theory is heavily based in genetics. The heritability of genes allows traits that survive to be passed from generation to generation. The strongest version of an evolutionary-cognitive explanation of religion requires that religion, and presumably all cultural behavior, is the direct, linear result of genetically programmed, highly specific, innate, universal cognitive systems or modules. These genetic structures are presumed to be neurophysiologically expressed in cognitive modules. We have already suggested that the evidence for a strong claim of modular mental mechanisms is rather weak. And theories of how these hypothesized mental modules might be linked to genotypes (the underlying genetic structure) which are then so directly expressed neurophysiologically are hard to come by. Often the issue of spelling out the actual linkages between genes, neurophysiological structures in the brain, and cognition is ignored in favor of a simple assertion of these connections. But insistence on such tight linkages, which are so necessary to strongly connect Neo-Darwinian evolution to cognitive activity, becomes increasingly difficult as we discover that the phenotypes (the actual traits a person possess—eye color, hair color, etc.) do not map directly, in a linear fashion onto the genotypes (the individual's genes).

While writers on cognitive psychological explanations of culture and religion frequently pull back from claims of "genetic determinism," in reality their arguments often require very strong causal links between evolution, which works on genes; then between the resulting genotypes and the organism's neurophysiological structures; and then between these neurophysiological modules and cognitive activities. But a direct causal link between heritable genes and their genotypes and the resultant phenotypes, especially in the area of cognition, is increasingly being questioned. For example, Day in his 2007 article reviews several lines of research that call into question any direct, linear connection of genotype, phenotype, and complex human behaviors and cultural institutions. Rather, research finds that relations between these domains are too open to support claims of direct causation. Day points out that in biological domains, including neurology, *physically distinct* molecular structures may generate identical, or near-identical *functional properties*" (emphasis in original). He cites examples of amino acids in which their properties are the same but their underlying molecular structure is different. A neurological example: when part of the brain becomes dysfunctional through trauma or disease, sometimes another part, not originally associated with the diminished area's function, can take that function over and perform it. In other words, the connection between genetic structure and physical or psychological function is not necessary direct. Of course there are links here but they may not be as hard and fast as required for a strong argument for neo-Darwinian evolution as the sole or even primary source of explanation for human cultural behavior. As Day concludes, "the goal of finding bridge laws that will allow us to reduce one enterprise (psychology) to another (neuroscience) and, thereby articulate nomological generalizations [i.e., scientific laws] about human cognition, is a fantasy."

Instead of reducing culture and religion to genetics, which is the core of Darwinian theory, there is increasing evidence for a more two-way, reciprocal model of the relationship between genes and culture. Culture may impact the genotype-phenotype connection as much, if not more, than the inherited genotype directly gives rise to culture. Genetics is not determinative. Genes that exist may be inert. To become active, genes must be "expressed." But gene expression can be influenced by the organism's interaction with its environment. Research now finds that throughout our lives, our environmental interactions modify these genetic structures and how they are expressed.

For example, some fruit flies have a gene that results in winglessness, but when environmental temperature was raised by 10 degrees, the gene was not expressed and wings appeared. Some mice have a gene for high blood pressure but it is expressed only if mice are nursed by their natural mothers. When nursed by unrelated females, the gene is not expressed. Or when mice with a genotype for obesity were given a diet heavy in methyl-rich vitamins like folic acid, B-12, etc., they did not develop any obesity or other irregularities; while their genetically identical siblings, given a standard mouse diet, did. The methyl group inhibited the expression of the obesity genes. So it seems that culture and behavior might influence genetics as much as genetics influences culture and behavior. If that proves correct, then claiming there is a single deterministic causal arrow from genes to phenotype to cognition, as required by a strong argument for evolutionary explanations of cognition and behavior, may be vastly oversimplified.

Evolutionary cognitive science insists that the mind evolved as it did *only* to solve problems arising from navigating the physical environment and replicating one's genes. Cultural

phenomena are by-products of the drive to survive and propagate one's genotype. This assumption is central in every evolutionary explanation of cultural phenomena like religion.
Everything must be linked back, directly or indirectly, to surviving and reproducing. This is the basis for the insistence
that the cognitive structures that give rise to religion evolved
for other, nonreligious purposes. Religion only "hijacks"
them. But what evidence is there that our hunter-gatherer
ancestors were concerned only with, as I say to my students,
the "three Fs"—"feeding, fighting, and ... ah ... reproducing"? Of course we don't know. It is at best a hypothesis based
on an interpretation of a Darwinian theory that insists that
survival and reproduction must be our only basic drives. This
is all conjecture. We have absolutely no evidence to support it.
Yet the debunking use of evolutionary cognitive science rests
on this claim.

Actually the evidence we do have points in a very different
direction. As far back as anthropologists can go into the lives of
our earliest stone-age ancestors we find evidence of art, music,
and religion. We have cave illustrations of geometric shapes,
hand prints, and perhaps sketches of animal forms from over
40,000 years ago, and flutes that have survived from about the
same period. This very dating suggests to some researchers that
this art might have been produced by Neanderthals rather than
Homo sapiens. And some are convinced that the Neanderthals
also made music and engaged in dance, although there is no way
to demonstrate that. But we do know they buried their dead in
ways suggestive of a belief in the afterlife. Then, of course, there
is the stunning cave art in the Grotte de Chauvet in France that
may date back about 36,000 years. The art work is genuinely
breathtaking and sophisticated, not at all primitive or childish.
There is evidence that ritual activity also occurred in those caves,
and anthropological studies of contemporary hunter-gatherer

cultures in Australia found they produced rock paintings as part of elaborate religious rituals.

Most striking for our purposes is the Gobekli Tepe temple in Southern Turkey; a series of concentric circles made from massive stone pillars with intricately carved bas-reliefs of hosts of animals. While many millennia after the cave paintings, Gebekli Tepe is many millennia earlier than Stonehenge or the Great Pyramids. It may well have been constructed by hunter-gatherers or those just beginning the transition to settled agriculture who were able to neatly cut, shape, and transport sixteen-ton stones with no wheels or domesticated animals to help. There is no evidence of settled living around the site and the dating puts it back to the time of foraging. How basically nomadic peoples constructed this site remains one of the many inexplicable things about. All the evidence suggests this was a ceremonial site that required a great deal of social organization to construct and maintain. This led the editors of *National Geographic* to write "We used to think agriculture gave rise to cities and later to writing, art, and religion. Now the world's oldest temple suggests that the urge to worship sparked civilization." So it seems our hunter-gatherer ancestors were interested in more than the 3 Fs. The evidence suggests that from their earliest days, hominids devoted themselves to art, music, and spirituality as well as to surviving and reproducing. None of this directly contradicts the evolutionary hypotheses on which the cognitive science of religion draws in explaining religion. But it does imply that a picture of primitive hunter-gatherers whose cognitive capacities were being selected *only* for survival and reproduction and of religion later arising by "hijacking" those capacities is grossly oversimplified.

This point is crucial here. The debunkers' case rests on the idea that religion is the by-product of cognitive mechanisms that evolved for totally different functions, that is, for the sake of survival and reproduction. That is what enables them to claim that religion "hijacks" these cognitive capacities whose "true" use is for survival and reproduction. Of course science, art, politics, and all culture, on this view, piggy-back or hijack these cognitive mechanisms. So that is not necessarily a problem. But there is a deeper problem here. How do we know that these cognitive capacities evolved *only* for survival and reproduction? The truth is we don't. No evidence is offered here to support that assertion. It is an assumption. Arising from current neo-Darwinian theory projected backwards onto the process of evolution, this assumption that survival and reproduction are life's only primary motivations is a figment of the contemporary Darwinian model of human nature. It may be correct, but there is little evidence to support it. As we have said, what evidence there is points in a different direction. While survival and reproduction are crucial to the species, from the beginning hominids have made music, created art, engaged in ritual and religious practice. Whatever their evolutionary trajectory, and that is lost to us, there is no reason not to see them being as much a part of our early heritage as sex and gathering food. They are not hijacks on our basic nature, they are part of our basic nature.

There is, however, an additional logical problem with these broad and general evolutionary explanations as deployed in the cognitive science of religion and other cultural phenomena. The idea of the "survival of the fittest," as we indicated before, is basically a tautology. Who are the fittest? Those who survive. How do we know they are the fittest? Because they survived. This is just a definition of what is meant by "the fittest." Pure tautologies have no explanatory or predictive power. Decisions about who is the fittest are always made after the fact, when we see who survived. Nothing is predicted. If we ask: Why did they survive? And the answer is: Because they were the fittest. And we ask: But what that tells us? The answer can only be to repeat: "They survived." No new information is added. Pure tautologies are therefore compatible with any outcome. They can explain any result.

For a long time, it was argued that mothers protected their children because that guaranteed the passing on of their genes. Then a decade ago we had an unhappy rash of mothers killing their newborns. They were all unmarried teenagers. Without being asked, a colleague quickly explained that these young girls wanted to wait until they had better prospects for mating and childrearing and therefore better opportunities for passing on their genes. That could be true. But a theory that can cover two totally opposed outcomes, and is therefore unfalsifiable, is hard to call strictly scientific. No one denies that over time the fittest are those that survive and propagate, partly because that is what being the fittest means. Just like, over time, the best teams probably win. That is because winning over time is what being the best means. By itself it is a very general description of a course of events; it is not necessarily an explanation of why that specific course of events happened. The biologist and philosopher Holmes Rolston writes bluntly,

> It now becomes hard to ensure that the theory [of natural selection] is not trivial or circular, that is, that the survival of the fittest does not reduce to the survival of those fittest to survive ... natural selection readily accommodates such an enormous variety of observations that we begin to wonder whether this part really is immune from testing. ... That the best adapted survive is not surprising; it is inevitable. ... Natural selection characterizes every reasonably

imaginable course that might have been taken.... Thus, it
is no accident that the principle cannot predict anything,
covering, as it does, everything that eventuates or might
have eventuated.... All this can seem quite plausible, and
testifies to the explanatory power of natural selection. But
meanwhile it becomes difficult conceive of observations
that could defeat the theory.... What explains too much,
explains nothing.

My point is not in any way to criticize those models of the process of speciation that draw upon population genetics and the
heritability of traits. Clearly genotypes do vary and those that
survive are passed along. I certainly affirm that the "survival of
the fittest" clearly describes why some species survive—such as
the fastest tigers and the tallest giraffes—and some do not in the
biological domain. And the genotype associated with the tiger's
power and the giraffe's neck can be traced throughout various
populations of tigers and giraffes and shown to be associated
with their higher rates of reproduction. That is all good science.
But these accounts work as explanations and not just reports
of a course of events because the genetic links seem clear. But
practicing a religion, or studying physics, or organizing a political movement are much more complex, and the genetic links
much looser, and therefore less connected to evolutionary survival, which only applies to genotypes, than a tiger's muscles or
a giraffe's neck. So it is worth thinking carefully about just how
much additional explanatory power and new empirical data we
achieve when we apply a very generalized covering theory like
the notion of evolutionary survival to complex cultural phenomena like religion. It might be shown to be quite a lot, especially
when religion is grossly oversimplified to a few intellectual
propositions; or it might turn out to be primarily a tautological
description.

Does Cognitive Science Not Just Explain but Also Refute Religion?

In the end, how compelling is the debunkers' "explanation" of religion and how convincing are their claims to have decisively refuted it?

If we think there is a God because of an oversensitive agency-detection module and that there is a soul as well as a body because our physical-exploration module is only loosely coupled to our psychological-awareness module, does that eliminate these beliefs from our lives? Does that end the matter of religion right there? The crusaders against religion insist that the answer must be yes. But is that insistence reasonable?

Of course, it depends on what they mean by it. If they are making a very strong claim that these universal cognitive structures cause a person to believe in God or the soul, so that these beliefs are entirely determined by these unconscious cognitive processes, then they have created a logical conundrum for themselves. The religious person is logically entitled to reply that "the only reason that you say that I believe in God because of my unconscious cognitive processes is because of your unconscious cognitive processes. If my beliefs are only the result of my unconscious cognitive processes, then yours must be only the result of yours. If that is reason enough not to take my beliefs seriously then it is reason enough not to take yours seriously either." This is a discussion that will end in a stalemate and get nowhere.

And that is not, in fact, what cognitive psychology says. This literature consistently maintains that with effort our explicit, more rational cognitive capabilities can analyze and overrule the more implicit, intuitive processes that often drive our conscious reflections. That is actually what the crusaders call on us to do in the case of religious beliefs, to use the reasoning they supply us with to overrule our natural tendency to believe religious fictions. But, of course, there is no reason why analogous critical reasoning processes cannot be used to analyze, and maybe overrule, the tacit processes that drive the debunkers' conscious claims and arguments. So we are back to the question that runs throughout this book regarding the basic background assumptions and intuitive sensibilities that underlie either the debunkers' claims or those of the religiously committed.

To make the claim that their accounts must, logically and necessarily, undermine belief in God, the debunkers would have to demonstrate that our normal "theory of mind" and perception of causality, which they see as the cognitive bases for our religious beliefs, are always and everywhere mistaken and can never be relied on. But of course that is clearly not true. We meet other human beings and they certainly seem to us to possess minds, feelings, intentions. We are not led astray by our "theory of mind," unless you believe "mind" is an illusion. Likewise, with our belief in causal connections. In scientific research, medical diagnosis, and everyday life we rely on a belief in causation all the time. Regarding religion, the debunkers' assumption seems to be that if a belief is the result of natural selection, it cannot also be true. But obviously our beliefs in other persons or in causality are, according to these theories, the result of natural selection, and they are also correct. Of course, we can sometimes be mistaken about such things; but deciding when that occurs is an empirical or philosophical question, not one within the scope of evolutionary psychology. And we have argued at length, and it is widely acknowledged, that accounts of the origin of beliefs by themselves tell us little or nothing about the truth of those beliefs.

A stronger version of this argument says that our beliefs in gods and souls result from cognitive mechanisms like HADD and "folk psychology," which are notoriously biased toward giving us false positives. That makes them so radically unreliable that little or nothing that results from them can be true. How compelling is that?

First, this argument assumes that the *only* reason a person holds such beliefs is because of those supposedly unreliable cognitive mechanisms. We have already examined that argument and found it wanting. Even if it were true that these cognitive mechanisms do partially generate such beliefs, nothing from cognitive science could necessarily or logically prove that those mechanisms were the *only* cause for these beliefs. No reasons or evidence are given that demonstrate that our religious beliefs can have only one cause. So even if the cognitive mechanisms involved were shown to be totally unreliable, that would not entail that other, more reliable factors were not also involved. Again, demonstrating the existence of psychological causes for a belief does not necessarily eliminate other reasons for holding it.

Second, let us, for the sake of argument, grant what I do not think is necessarily true and say that the originating causes for religious beliefs are heavily biased toward false positives. The question of false positives is one that sometimes bedevils medical diagnosis. Suppose we have a blood test for a particularly virulent form of cancer where biopsies done on the supposedly cancerous tissue after surgery revealed a high rate of false positives. That is, many patients were positive on the blood test but after the tissue was removed and biopsied, it was often found free of cancer. Still, some patients had cancer and would have died had the surgery not been done. How much weight should a physician give to the blood test results, given its high rate of false positives, in her recommendation for or against surgery?

This example suggests two things relevant to the cognitive science of religion. First, in matters of ultimate concern, such as life and death or maybe ultimate truths, it might be reasonable to rely on methods even they have a high probability of false positives. To the extent that you think that the existence of God or some ultimate power is a matter of ultimate concern, it might be reasonable to downplay the importance of false positives. This would be bit analogous to Pascal's famous wager. So even if we grant what I think is a false premise, that our agency-detection processes are so biased as to be almost totally unreliable, that does not automatically mean we should not rely on them in special cases.

Second, in the case of the cancer test, the biopsies provided very strong, reasonably objective evidence for the rate of false positives. But in the case of HADD there is no such reasonably objective test to assess whether it is giving us false positives in the domain of "supernatural agents." We could hypothetically assess the rate of false positives in domains like whether noises in the grass are lions or rocks are bears or noises at night are intruders. But obviously, in reality the claim that HADD is biased toward a high number of false positives is not the result of a standardized, relatively objective measure like a biopsy. Rather it is a projection of evolutionary cognitive psychological speculations about HADD's existence back in time and of a physicalist viewpoint that denies, in the first place, the existence of any spiritual or sacred realities. As we said before, in our ordinary life we usually easily detect such false positives (there is no intruder in the basement) and dismiss them. So the claim about HADD's hypothesized rate of false positives may be much weaker than the debunkers acknowledge.

There is another version of the argument that claims that cognitive science demonstrates that our evolved cognitive mechanisms would serve up to us a belief in God and in a spiritual part of human nature even in the absence of a God or a soul. That is the real reason we believe in such things; there is no other reason. Clearly this is what a physicalist must say. For the physicalist there is no God and so this argument that our cognition alone creates such a belief describes the actual situation. Of course, for the religious person, this is not the reality. For them there really is a God and there are reasons independent of the operation of HADDs and other such mechanisms, to believe in God. How to decide?

The verification of religious claims and the validity of reasons offered for them is obviously way beyond the scope of this book. Armies of books have been marshaled on all sides of that question. Even a cursory review would require at least another whole book. I would only offer two stipulations here: (1) religious beliefs will be verified only in the larger context of a religious frame of reference, just as the existence of quarks can be verified only in the context of contemporary physics or the reality of curved space can be verified only in the context of the Theory of Relativity; and (2) the validity of that larger, religious frame of reference will be decided primarily on pragmatic grounds in the two senses described earlier. The validity of the frame of reference will depend on its capacity to perform functions that we value; and that there will be some things we will not understand unless we practice them.

The debunkers might say instead that if we think there is a God because of an overactive agency-detection module and that there is a soul as well as a body because our physical-exploration module is only loosely coupled to our psychological-awareness module, this still should eliminate these beliefs from our lives. This does indeed end the matter of religion right there because even if there were other explanations for why a person believes in God, we should always and only prefer the physicalist explanation. The debunkers seem to feel that since a physicalist account of religion can be given, it should trump and all other accounts. Is that really the case?

We noted much earlier that all explanations are incomplete: they contain assumptions that are not demonstrable and must simply be accepted; they focus on some aspects of the phenomenon under consideration, in this case the origin of religion, and inevitably overlook or ignore other aspects. So physicalist explanations cannot simply claim to be complete and leave it there. We have listed several reasons for not considering reductive physicalist explanations to be always compelling or complete. So simply insisting that we must prefer physicalist explanations because they are the most compelling may be very convincing if you have already committed yourself to a physicalist outlook and your intuitive sensibilities push you in a physicalist direction. But that insistence may not be so convincing if you are skeptical about physicalism as a total worldview.

The reason I've most often heard for preferring physicalist explanations is that they are in line with science. That is true up to a point. Natural science does seek to explain occurrences on the basis of physical causes, although the description of what constitutes "the physical" has greatly expanded since the time of Newton. That is a necessary methodological principle of physical science. And contemporary biological science, and some social sciences, take place within an evolutionary framework. These are necessary background assumptions for doing natural science today. But assuming these things as a precondition for doing science does not entail that they are the only valid outlook on the world or that doing science is the only thing worth doing. Science does not say that science is the only valid way to approach the world. Some scientists may insist that is true but science itself does not require such a large claim. Many scientists reject it. And, as we have said, it is not an empirical claim at all. It is an assumption, a belief held by some. But it is not necessary for the conduct of science. Rejecting this claim does not make one antiscientific. One can reject a singularly physicalist worldview and still do scientific work and appreciate scientific research.

In the first part of his 2008 book, Edward Slingerland reviews much of the same material as I have from the philosophy of science; and he comes to a similar conclusion when he writes, "if we take underdetermination seriously, we cannot claim for physicalist explanations some sort of a priori superiority over religious ones.... In this respect Feyerabend is correct that modern Western science enjoys no formal epistemological advantage over traditional religion." But Slingerland is clearly unhappy with this conclusion. He desperately wants to grant natural science an epistemologically privileged *carte blanche* and not just in its areas of expertise; and therefore to privilege the very physicalism which his earlier discussion undermined. His reasons for insisting that we should always privilege physicalist explanations are pragmatic. He writes "The ultimate defense of physicalist over religious explanations, at least at the macro level of everyday, observable objects, is thus a pragmatic one: physicalist explanations so far seem to work better." But he provides no sense of context for these large generalizations. Of course Newton's laws are the best (only?) account for calculating the length of a shadow or the coming and going of the tides in front of our home. But they tell me nothing about whether I have a moral responsibility for the state of the ocean.

So his final defense of physicalism is pragmatic. But it is a very narrow form of pragmatism. When he lists the pragmatic goals that undergird physicalism, virtually all his examples are either technological products or medical advancements. Are gadgets and good health the only human goods? There is no recognition that someone might want to learn to appreciate a Bach cantata or a piece by Philip Glass, or to explore another culture through literature, or to follow the Delphic prescription and "know thyself" through various psychotherapeutic processes, or work at solving complex mathematical puzzles unrelated to the laboratory; to say nothing of investigating in a disciplined way the possibility of a "deeper" or more encompassing source of self and cosmos through philosophy and contemplation. It is no coincidence that a purely physicalist position articulates only the most concrete physical products as the goals of life, and that such claims arise in the most materialistic culture in history. Physicalism is not made more compelling by continually incanting "physicalism works better." Slingerland defines truth as "the successful achievement of goals," but the only goals he seems to allow are those compatible with a physicalist outlook. A circular argument if ever I saw one. So his pragmatic reasons for always preferring physicalist explanations come down to always preferring a life of material commodities.

Slingerland also briefly claims that the basic issue of the "underdetermination of theory by data," which decisively undercuts the positivist approach, can be defeated by "Occam's razor," the principle that the simplest explanation should be preferred and that one should not have "too many" explanatory principles. Yet he clearly and correctly recognizes that "Occam's razor" is hardly a definitive rule, but rather is "essentially a pragmatic heuristic, whether and how it is applied depends on unformalized hunches about how many is 'too many' and a probabilistic sense of what is reasonable." So in the end his pragmatic defense of positivism and physicalism comes down to saying "The slippery slide down the underdetermination slope is blocked by a collection of hunches, prejudices, and intellectual values that have evolved as part of human cognitive architecture. It is these intuitions that organize our experience of the world, play a major role in determining the sorts of hypotheses we can formulate, and help us decide between competing hypotheses." Ironically, evolved cognitive mechanisms are cited positively when they can be twisted in support of physicalism; but these are the same kinds of mechanisms that are vigorously dismissed when they support religion! And this sounds very much like the idea that our basic epistemological claims rest upon a judgment ("decid(ing) between competing hypotheses") that I have also insisted on throughout this text. Such a final appeal to judgment, then, can support religious outlooks at least as strongly as physicalist ones.

Slingerland refers to that "collection of hunches, prejudices, and intellectual values that have evolved as part of human cognitive architecture" as common sense. He is eager to grant such "common sense" a "genuine epistemological power." And he seems to assume that "common sense" always favors a narrow empiricism and physicalism, since "common sense" is "natural, found cross culturally"; just like religion on this view. The invocation of common sense has a complex history in thinking about religion. Slingerland claims that common sense supports a reductive empiricism that leaves little or no place for religious belief. On the other hand, the Scottish philosopher Thomas Reid developed what he called a "common sense" philosophy whose goal was to support religious belief on what he took to be its firm foundation in common sense. Justin Barrett has argued that cognitive science supports Reid's claim that common sense favors and supports religious belief. So invoking it as evidence for reductive empiricism is, at best, an ambiguous move. Judgment and common sense, on which Slingerland rests his preference for physicalist accounts, have historically been powerful sources of support for religious beliefs.

Once more regarding the question that seems to me to be at the heart of the antireligious crusaders use of cognitive science. If we think there is a God because of an overactive agency-detection module and that there is a soul as well as a body because our physical-exploration module is only loosely coupled to our psychological-awareness module, does that eliminate these beliefs from our lives? Does that end the matter of religion right there? The crusaders against religion insist that the answer must be yes. But is that insistence reasonable?

We might ask, if we think that events in the world have causes because a causal-detection module is at work, does that mean we should eliminate that belief from our life? The answer is obviously no. We depend on that belief in almost everything we do; diagnose a disease, get our car repaired, or check the circuit breaker when the lights go out. Such a belief helps us immeasurably in finding our way around the physical world. Just as the basic sense that causality operates in the physical world is confirmed by our regular reliance on it to find our way around the ordinary world, so our religious sensibilities can help us find our way around the moral world. And, if we choose to engage in it, they can help us find our way around the spiritual world, the world of prayer, worship, service, and the love of wisdom.

So the fact that cognitive science finds that some religious beliefs arise from the activity of supposedly universal cognitive tendencies does not entail that those beliefs are necessarily false; nor does it compel anyone to give them up. If all beliefs in all domains result from underlying cognitive mechanisms, then that fact in itself is not a cause for rejecting a set of beliefs. So then, how should we decide which to hold and which to fold? It should be clear by now that cognitive science suggests that our conscious deliberations and judgments are often driven by unconscious cognitive processes. But that those tacit processes can be made conscious and themselves become the object of deliberation and decision, a process that will, of course, also arise from tacit, cognitive underpinnings. So again we come back to the point which has been central to this book regarding the importance of evaluating as much as possible these tacit sensibilities and background judgments. This is a question we will take up in the final chapter.

Conclusion

My point in this chapter is certainly not to "deny the theory of evolution," certainly not to reject the descent of one species from another. My point is simply to raise some questions about how much interpretive gain is really gained by the use of evolutionary theory in the explanation of religion. I am not denying any connections between an inherited genotype, the individual's phenotype (and in this case their neurophysiology), and their behavior. My point is only to wonder if all these connections are really as direct and as strong as is necessary to use evolution, which works only on the genotype, to provide a very complete explanation of religious belief and behavior. Nor am I arguing that reductive physicalism, which believes that the physical world is the only reality and that natural science is the only arbiter of truth, is necessarily false. I am just saying that good reasons can be given for thinking that it is false. It is not irrational to think that. So the three pillars of the crusaders' debunking interpretations of the cognitive science of religion—that is a singularly reductive physicalist view of the world, the sole reliance on a positivistic methodology that insists on natural science as the only valid path to knowledge, and a belief that evolutionary accounts can explain everything important about human life—may not be as compelling as they presuppose. Without going to the absurd extreme of some pious devotees and rejecting the scientific method and its findings altogether, perhaps the religiously inclined should have the courage of their convictions and insist on a recognition of the limits and the incompleteness of a solely physicalist viewpoint, a narrowly positivistic methodology, and a possible overgeneralization of Darwinian constructs.

Chapter 4

Beyond Reductive Physicalism

Mind and Nature

So far we have argued that the use of cognitive science to debunk or refute religious claims or even significantly to "explain" religion is not particularly convincing for at least three reasons:

(1) It has not explained religion in any comprehensive way. At most it has given an account of a few isolated beliefs, taken out of context, that hardly sum up to a fully functioning religious tradition.

(2) The argument that the explanations it has proffered have refuted religious claims is not logically compelling since it is generally agreed that showing the reasons why a person comes to hold a set of beliefs entails nothing about the truth or falsity of those beliefs.

(3) The debunking use of cognitive science, I have argued, depends on interpreting its findings in a narrow and reductive physicalist context, and there are many reasons to question the adequacy of that sort-of physicalist worldview.

So where does that leave the cognitive scientific study of religion? If a narrow, reductive physicalism is questionable, and all accounts, including those of contemporary cognitive science, are incomplete, there is no reason to think that a reductive physicalist account of the natural world, including humanity, is complete or correct. As a matter of fact, there are many reasons to think it is not.

I want discuss just one reason that suggests that a reductive physicalism is not correct, which I alluded to before and which grows out of my own work in the field of behavioral medicine. In order to eliminate all other possible explanations for religious belief except those provided by evolutionary cognitive science, the debunkers have to insist on the strongest possible causal influence from the lower, primarily unconscious, level of cognitive processes to the conscious level of religious belief. This causal influence must flow in only one direction, from the lower levels to the higher. This is often called "bottom-up" causation and is a necessary element in any theory that wants to insist that our conscious beliefs are but the product of our unconscious cognitive mechanisms. This creates a serious contradiction at the heart of their argument. Claiming that implicit cognitive mechanisms alone explain religious belief requires a virtually deterministic causal connection between them. But then, the debunkers appeal to us to use our conscious cognitive powers to alter or eliminate these religious beliefs and the implicit cognitions that cause them. However, if all our conscious cognitions are causally determined by implicit, unconscious cognitive mechanisms, that would not be possible, and making that appeal would be an act of consummate irrationality. On the other hand, if it is possible for our conscious cognitive activity to alter or overrule our unconscious, implicit cognitive mechanisms, then the relationship between the implicit and explicit levels is much more complex than the cognitive science of religion, especially in its debunking forms, suggests. And the claim that unconscious cognitive processes can completely explain our conscious religious beliefs is severely undermined.

Any ability of our conscious, higher-level cognitive processes, our thoughts, intentions, and feelings to influence lower-level mechanisms, would complicate the picture immensely. This, often called "top-down" causation, would spell the end of any claim that our thoughts, beliefs, and feelings are determined only by more basic cognitive or neurological mechanisms. And that would undermine the argument that the only reasonable way to understand our conscious thoughts and intentions is by analyzing their mainly unconscious antecedents. Most cognitive and neuroscientists today insist that is the case. That conscious thoughts, feelings, and choices are entirely caused by lower-level cognitive mechanisms. And that they are, in turn, entirely caused by neurological activity going on in the brain. That is, they insist there is only bottom-up causation; top-down mental causation is a myth. I want to suggest otherwise. I will insist that both logic and evidence support the strongest possible model of top-down conscious causation.

Any insistence that there is only bottom-up causation, and that everything we think and do is entirely caused by unconscious cognitive and neurological mechanisms, seems clearly incompatible with every religious, and even nonreligious but humanistic, understandings of human persons. So religious philosophers and their nonreligious humanistic counterparts would seem compelled to argue for some type of top-down causation; or else face the fact that most, if not all, of what they treasure about human nature—its capacity for moral responsibility, for complex and creative thought, for transcendental states of consciousness—is just froth on waves of neurons and evolved cognitive mechanisms. This is another area of obvious tension between religious convictions and much current, popular neuroscience. Here the nonreligious humanist and religious person seem faced with three unhappy alternatives: reject science, try to find a place for humanistic and religious concerns within the claims made by contemporary neuroscientists, or argue that neuroscience does not, in fact, have the antireligious, antihumanistic impact often attributed to it by those who want to use it to debunk religion. Rejecting science in any comprehensive way, or affirming claims that directly contradict well-researched scientific findings, as opposed to physicalist interpretations of scientific findings, are not options for me. So I will consider the second and third alternatives. And that discussion will build on what I think is one of the strongest arguments against a narrow and reductive physicalism, and maybe all forms of physicalism, drawing on work in behavioral medicine.

Nonreductive Physicalism

In the previous chapter I offered a series of arguments against a narrow, reductive physicalism, since I think that position, or something very close to it, drives the debunking interpretations of cognitive science. But that is not the only form of what is called physicalism today. In this chapter, I want to look at other versions of physicalism and discuss some of their implications for interpreting cognitive science in relation to religion. Some claim that a revised form of physicalism, called "nonreductive physicalism," can affirm the moral and religious life and find a place for them within the theories of contemporary neuroscience. Rather than eliminating the features of human life on which religion depends, as a reductive physicalism would, this form of physicalism affirms, in the words of the theologian and philosopher of science Nancey Murphy, that "consciousness and religious awareness are emergent properties and they have top-down causal influence on the body." This position's most famous spokesman, the Nobel laureate Roger Sperry, enthuses, "The long-banned subjective states and qualities are now put up front—in the driver's seat as it were."

Arguments in support of nonreductive physicalism must go beyond simply describing the functioning of neural organizations or pointing out correlations between conscious events and neuronal activity. Reductive physicalists, nonreductive physicalists, and dualists all agree about the functioning of various neurotransmitters, the growth and decay of neuronal cells, and which parts of the brain are more active or more quiescent during various mental activities. There is little dispute these days about these findings. They are a major part of the data of contemporary cognitive neuroscience and psychophysiology.

Nonreductive physicalism, like its cousin reductive physicalism and its antagonist dualism, are not simply reports of experimental findings. They are, rather, interpretations of these findings. For the most part, reductive physicalists, nonreductive physicalists, and even today's dualists (Popper & Eccles, Penfield) agree on the results of current neuroscience experiments. Their disagreements are about the interpretation of these findings. So these disagreements will probably not be settled by appeals to experimental data on which they all virtually agree, but rather to which position gives the most complete, coherent, and compelling account of those data.

Sometimes the category of "emergence" is added to the discourse of physicalism to make it nonreductive. The category of "emergence" has spawned a metaphysical vision of a hierarchical universe with the higher levels "emerging" from the lower ones. Such a metaphysical position has obvious applications to the problem of consciousness and mental causation. Roger Sperry writes that the central nervous system is "governed by novel emergent properties of its own." Consciousness is "no longer a mere impotent epiphenomenon of brain activity. It becomes a powerful impelling force in its own right." Conscious agency emerges from neuronal organization and then exercises control over it. This emergent power of consciousness necessitates a new model of causality which "combines traditional bottom-up with emergent top-down causation," in which mental activities "exert a concomitant supervenient form of downward control over their constituent neurocellular activities."

Often the metaphor of emergence, when used to conceptualize the relationship of the mind and the brain, performs two functions. First, it explicitly rejects reductionism as an explanatory strategy and insists that new levels of explanation are required to account for consciousness and intentionality. Calling phenomena emergent entails that a complete description cannot be given in terms of an underlying state of affairs. Lower-level laws and processes cannot completely predict the occurrence or behavior of the emergent reality. Thus, labeling consciousness "emergent" means that it cannot be completely explained in terms of neuronal processes. Restricted to explanations using only the categories of neurophysiology, the neurosciences can never completely explain domains that emerge out of, and therefore go beyond, sheer physiology. Second, the category of emergence can be used to refer not only to new explanatory categories, but also to new actual properties. On this position, mental properties are of a different nature than lower-level neurophysiological properties. They exercise a new type of causality, downward causation, that arises with this new emergent domain. Emergence means that something genuinely new, unique, and unpredictable can arise from within the natural order. Thus the reality of downward causation as an emergent property is affirmed. However in this discussion, there is little detailed specification of such how causality might work.

In the first instance, the category of emergence appears concerned with hierarchies of explanation, since the strongest arguments in its favor are that at each level of complexity within nature new categories of explanation are required. This is part of a much larger discussion in the philosophy of science about whether the theories of particular sciences can all be reduced to or derived from fundamental theories of physics. This seems highly unlikely. Chemistry requires categories beyond those of physics, biology requires categories beyond those of chemistry, and the study of consciousness requires categories that are necessarily psychological.

There is a clear tension here over the problem of continuity and discontinuity within nature. Science requires continuity within nature; but religion and spirituality require a degree of discontinuity in order to avoid a hard reductionism. The category of emergence is relied on to provide the necessary degree of discontinuity in order to make such realities as downward causation comprehensible. Sperry and other nonreductive physicalists clearly and forcefully maintain the reality of the spiritual domain and reject the kind of physicalism that drives the debunkers of religion within cognitive neuroscience. Rather, their paradigm recognizes that some notion of mental causation is a necessary component of any religious or humanistic outlook. The question that remains is whether their category of emergence can do all the work required of it, in order to affirm a robust model of mental causation.

What Needs to Be Explained?

Practicing and teaching behavioral medicine, and working directly at the interface of the body and the mind with suffering patients, gives me another perspective on the cognitive science-neuroscience and religion discussion. In brief, my argument will be that the physicalists' account of consciousness is simply not adequate in the face of the data of behavioral medicine. Physicalism, as currently formulated, cannot account for the following top-down activities of the mind.

Hypnosis. For several years I have practiced clinical hypnosis as part of my behavioral medicine work. I have found it particularly effective in the treatment of anxiety, chronic pain, stress-related disorders, and smoking cessation. My claims in this chapter go beyond clinical anecdotes. Hypnotic interventions have been extensively documented to be effective in these areas. Central to my own practice has been the use of imagery. For example, having a patient imagine they are warming their hands over a fire has been shown to increase the blood flow to their hands and so dilate blood vessels. This may help in relieving vascular headaches. Or, in reverse, having another patient imagine putting a hand in a bucket of cold water can induce numbness in the hand that can be transferred to other parts of the body and so serve to relieve chronic pain. It is common to remove warts by having the patient imagine them gone. Research has also documented that by using imagery under hypnosis, a person can impact their immune system's functioning. Brain scans of subjects undergoing hypnotic interventions for pain modulation and emotional arousal reveal consistent effects of hypnotic suggestions on the relevant brain centers.

It is hard to interpret such findings in any other way than as illustrating the power of mental imagery to affect the body. A person forms a purely inner mental act, an image, and the *following* result is that blood pressure changes, or pain sensations decrease, or other physiological processes alter. In light of such practices, it is hard for me to deny that inner mental activities can control physiological processes. The question for this chapter is the extent to which nonreductive physicalism can account for this.

Biofeedback. Biofeedback often uses interventions similar to those used in hypnosis. But biofeedback goes beyond clinical hypnosis in documenting the effects on the body. Employing imagery, direct instructions for calmness, and various relaxation techniques, biofeedback demonstrates under laboratory conditions that imagining a relaxed state, or heaviness in the limbs, or images of light or color, or prescinding from active thought can reduce heart rate, change skin conductance, relax muscular-skeletal tension, and even shift brain wave patterns.

The demonstrated capacity to control one's brain waves is theoretically interesting. Reductive physicalism, and perhaps all forms of physicalism, attribute primary causation to physical factors, that is, brain activity. It is certainly true that changes in electrical activity in the brain correlate with and may be said to cause mental activity in many circumstances. EEG biofeedback of electrical activity in the brain implies that under other conditions, understanding a set of instructions or forming a mental image comes first and is reliably *followed* by changes in patterns of brain activity.

In addition, brain scans comparing subjects visualizing an object with subjects actually seeing the object show differential blood flow to the visual cortex. Likewise, brain scans comparing hearing music played with a hypnotic hallucination of hearing music and simply imagining hearing the music show that imagining an experience produces a different neuronal pattern than actually having the experience. In all these cases, it would appear that mental activity, imagining a sound or an image, is the primary cause of changes in brain activity; and that one can learn to intentionally control one's brain waves and other neuronal activities.

Other clinical interventions also reveal the possibilities of consciously affecting one's neurophysiology. For example, studies have shown that consciously choosing to redirect attention and act against powerful compulsive urges not only effectively treats obsessive-compulsive disorder (OCD), but also modifies the underlying neuronal circuitry. Brain scans of patients successfully treated for OCD by such cognitive-behavioral treatments reveal significant changes in their cerebral physiology. Similar results have been shown in the treatment of depressed patients. Here too, active psychological interventions have produced measurable and significant alterations in cerebral activity directly attributable to intentional cognitive changes and reliably associated with relief from depression.

Physicalists insist that consciousness is only the result of cerebral functioning; however, the results of biofeedback, hypnosis, and brain scans of patients treated with active psychological interventions demonstrate that consciously choosing to form an image, redirect attention, refocus thoughts, or act differently, can directly affect basic cerebral activity. What is the cause and what is the effect here?

Meditation Research. Meditation-derived techniques have been increasingly deployed in the practice of behavioral medicine. The last two decades have witnessed an exponential increase in the number of articles detailing the psychophysiological effects of meditation. For some time the clinical literature has described the effectiveness of meditation-derived techniques for the treatment of anxiety disorders, stress, and more recently eating disorders, depression, and personality disorders. More recent psychophysiological research has demonstrated the impact of meditation on such basic physiological functions as brain hemispheric lateralization, immune-system functioning and emotional processing. Even short-term meditation practice has been shown to increase activity in the left cerebral hemisphere—a result associated with an increase in positive emotional responses—and improve immune functioning. More advanced meditators have demonstrated, under laboratory conditions, the ability to control fundamental physiological processes, such as basic reflexes, formerly thought to be beyond conscious control. Studies have also shown that a variety of cognitive processes can be altered through regular meditation practice. Meditation has been shown to dramatically improve the mind's ability to focus and maintain attention and to develop the capacity to detach from engrained emotional and cognitive reactions to familiar thoughts and feelings. This has been demonstrated to be important clinically in weakening and modifying long-standing patterns of anxious rumination, depressive thinking, addictive attachment, or reactive anger. Such meditation-based cognitive changes facilitate the emergence of self-regulatory functions that are experienced as healthier, saner, and more balanced. Thus the conscious choice to undertake a meditative discipline impacts a variety of physical and psychological domains.

Behavioral medicine appears to rule out a Cartesian dualism in which the mind or spirit are seen as disconnected from the body. It also seems to rule out an eliminativist physicalism in which mental activity is regarded as epiphenomenal and irrelevant to neurological and physiological functioning. At minimum it also sharpens the idea of "downward causation" and suggests that a rather strong notion of mental causation is essential to a complete understanding of the role of the mind. The kind of self-regulation currently being demonstrated in psychophysiological laboratories and clinical practice—involving hypnosis, biofeedback, and meditation—demands a robust account of mental causation. Certainly more robust than a reductive physicalism can supply.

Emergence and Downward Causation

Clearly, complex systems possess properties that their component parts do not: words, cells, and water have properties that emerge out of the organization of their letters, their macromolecules, or their atomic constitution. What, then, are some of the characteristics of an emergent property? At least three minimal conditions must be present so that something can be said to be an emergent property of a complex system. Let's call "A1" an emergent property of a system called "A." That would mean:

(1) A1 cannot exist without A.
(2) A1 has elements in common with A.
(3) A1 has characteristics or properties not possessed by the individual components of A.

(1) and (2) clearly describe the relation between words and letters. A word cannot exist without letters; both the letters and the word are linguistic, often written, forms. Or it describes the relation between a cell and its chemicals. A cell cannot exist apart from the chemicals; and the cell and the chemicals that make it up are both composed of atoms and molecules. It also describes the relationship between molecules of water and the atoms of hydrogen and oxygen. Water cannot exist apart from hydrogen and oxygen; and water and the two elements are all composed of subatomic particles.

However, if we say that consciousness is an emergent property of a system of physical neurons, we run into immediate problems.

(1) The claim that consciousness cannot exist apart from the brain is one of the things that such a model was supposed to demonstrate. An argument that begins by assuming this tenet may be simply circular and end up by concluding what it has already taken for granted. However, we might grant that consciousness may not exist apart from the brain in order to go on and explore the logic of this model. We must beware of using this model, however, to argue that consciousness cannot be separate

from the brain, since this model of emergent properties seems to depend on precisely this claim.

(2) This model of the mind emerging out of a system of physical neurons called the brain depends on the assumption that minds and brains are at least partially similar, so that they can be seen as aspects of a single interacting system. Calling this position a form of nonreductive physicalism underscores this assumption.

Are thoughts and neurons similar enough to be considered parts of the same system? That is the question faced by the nonreductive physicalist who uses the category of emergence. Consider:

(1) Neurons and other components of the central nervous system, like all physical entities, are always described in the categories of space and time. Thoughts and images are never described, except perhaps under poetic license, in terms of their mass, energy coefficient, or width.

(2) I may make a claim about the neurons in my brain—their number, density, organization, or development—and be mistaken about it. On the other hand, I cannot be mistaken about the ideas or sensations I have in my mind. If I say I feel a pain in my foot, I cannot be mistaken about feeling such a sensation, even if I do not have a foot.

If thoughts and neurons cannot be described in the same way, how similar are they really? On the other hand, thoughts and feelings do occur in time and space. And they are clearly correlated with physical activity in the central nervous system. Does that make them similar enough to physical entities for both to be considered parts of the same nonreductive, emergent physical system? That seems clearly to be a judgment call since good reasons can be offered on both sides of that question. That is why the problem is so controversial and these issues are so contested. To be considered part of the same system, thoughts and neurons need to be at least somewhat similar. Are thoughts similar enough to neurons to be understood as a property of a system of physical neurons? Certainly not in the same sense that a word can be understood as a system of letters or a cell as a system of chemicals.

Put most starkly, a thought is not a thing. The sensation of seeing red is not reducible to or translatable into statements about wavelengths, rods and cones, or neuronal processing. No description of physics or neurology can lead from there to a description of the experience of redness. They are simply two separate and distinct linguistic systems. One of the claimed advantages of the emergent model in contrast to dualism, is that it removes the dilemma of specifying how mind and brain, how spirit and matter are connected. Renaming consciousness as an emergent property may not account for the existence of consciousness without some way of specifying how two such very different things as thoughts and brains can be aspects of a single emergent system. Of course the nonreductive physicalist wants to claim that both thoughts and brains are, in some sense, physical. But my point is that specifying in exactly what sense images, thoughts, or intentions are themselves physical, as distinct from simply possessing physical correlates, is far from clear.

The model of emergent properties is supposed to be simpler than its competitors, but it is not clear in what sense this simplicity is a virtue if it provides no explanation of the process that most needs explaining, the connection of neuronal states and conscious states. As fervently as the proponents of this model might hope otherwise, it is not clear that just calling consciousness an emergent property removes the need, which dualism also has, to provide a theoretical bridge between brains and thoughts.

My concern here is not to take on the impossible task of answering all the questions and solve all the problems associated with the reality of mental causation. My only task here is to underscore the question, which is widely and hotly debated in the literature, as to whether any form of physicalism can handle the robust kind of mental causation I am alluding to. There are also emergentist thinkers that do not claim to be physicalist. Rather they describe themselves as providing a middle way between any form of physicalism and dualism. Obviously they do not fall under the critique I am offering here. They obviously accept my suggestion that all forms of physicalism have serious inadequacies when it comes to offering the fullest possible account of human existence. And they propose a more complex account of emergence than the minimalist model I have critiqued.

Of course, to the physicalist, the "folk psychological" account of mental causation is wrong to begin with. It depends on an ordinary model of "event" or "entity" being applied to the mental realm. And for the reductive physicalist, there are no actual mental entities or domains. There is only the physical domain that gives rise to the experience of a mental life. And that experience of a mental life is really a physical reality, even though it cannot be exhaustively described in physical categories and even though it requires subjective language to communicate itself. But then again, we seem to be back to the earlier discussion of the sense in which thoughts and intentions can be said to be physical, something nonreductive physicalism demands, given their obvious differences?

In these discussions of downward causation in relation to the category of emergence there can be confusion between categories of explanation and of causal agency. Most neuroscientists, even most physicalists, agree that higher-order cognitive processes can be described only in categories that go beyond simple accounts of neuronal firings and neurotransmitter releases or synaptic organization. These higher-order cognitive and psychological processes require higher-level categories. I agree that is a sufficient reason for adopting the metaphors of emergence in our descriptions of mental processes, as opposed to a hard reductionist position. But, as Dennis Bielfeldt writes, "Semantic irreducibility does not entail causal autonomy." That is, the category of emergence adequately describes the relationship between *levels of explanation* required in our accounts of conscious mental life. But it may not be adequate for a robust theory of mental causation.

Awareness

Many authors (Chalmers, Hutto, Nagel, Velmans) suggest that the real problem of consciousness involves not simply its contents, but rather the brute fact of awareness itself. Contrary to the physicalists' theory, it is not so easy to see how awareness itself can be completely mapped neurophysiologically.

Consider the following thought experiment. It is probably not possible in practice, but it is easy enough to visualize. Suppose you are on an operating table with your brain exposed, and a series of cameras and screens allow you to observe your own brain functioning. Since the brain itself carries little sensation, neurosurgery can be done with the patient awake. You notice the color red in the corner of the room, and at the same time you become aware of the neuronal discharge that represents the visual experience of seeing red. And you realize that the neuronal activity in the visual cortex is connected to the experience of seeing red. And simultaneously you notice the neuronal discharge that represents drawing the connection between the previous occipital activity and the experience of redness. And then, or perhaps simultaneously, you see the neuronal correlate of drawing the conclusion that the previous neuronal activity represents drawing the conclusion about the experience of redness. And of course there would have to be a neuronal correlate of that conclusion; but again, where in the sequence would you see it? And where would you see the neuronal correlate of seeing that?

Why is this so confusing? Because you are watching your brain record the experience of watching your brain record the experience of watching your brain . . . ad infinitum. You see the brain configuration change as you think new thoughts, but what do you see that goes with the recognition that you are watching the brain configuration change as you think new thoughts? What neuronal activity would you observe that goes with the awareness of your awareness?

It is hard to imagine mapping an increasing, hypothetically infinite, series of hierarchies onto the shifting linear configurations of neuronal activities, when one of these hierarchies represents an awareness of those shifting configurations of neuronal activities and another hierarchy represents an awareness of that awareness of those shifting configurations. What is the state of the system that goes with observing that state of the system? Nonreductive physicalists' models may not do away with the paradoxical relation between cortical states and conscious experiences, especially when the conscious experience in question is of the cortical state that goes with that conscious experience of that cortical state.

Can Nonreductive Physicalism Explain Top-Down Causality?

Obviously I agree with the nonreductive physicalist's assertion of top-down causality from mind to brain and then from brain to the other physiological systems that comprise the human being. This is a fundamental assumption of psychoneuroimmunology. And it is required to distinguish nonreductive from reductive physicalism. My concern is whether even the strongest nonreductive physicalist theory can really provide a sufficiently powerful model of top-down causality to explain the findings of psychophysiology.

Nonreductive physicalism insists on a conjunction between two levels of natural phenomena, mind and brain, or two sets of properties, mental and physical, without having to specify the exact nature of these levels or properties, except to say they can only occur in conjunction with one another. And, in addition, that one level is not easily, or not at all reducible to the other. That is, consciousness can occur only in conjunction with a physical brain, but it cannot be reduced to a description of neurons and neurotransmitters. Often the term "supervenience" is called on to do most of the explanatory work here. For example, the characteristics of water (its fluidity, ability to freeze or boil, etc.) supervene on its molecular structure. Presumably, any element that had that exact chemical composition (H_2O) would have the same properties. But these characteristics cannot be described by descriptions of oxygen or hydrogen alone. Or the meaning of a sentence supervenes on the sounds of its words. Presumably, any sentences that sounded alike would have the same meaning. But the meaning cannot be described simply by descriptions of the phonetics of the sound. Or the beauty of the *Mona Lisa* supervenes on the arrangements of the pigments that compose it. And any similarly arranged set of pigments would be as beautiful. But that beauty cannot be described in terms of the chemistry of pigments alone. Note that so defined, supervenience describes a nonreductive relationship that simply requires conjunction and not causality. The supervening properties cannot be descriptively reduced to the categories applied to the lower-level properties. But that does not necessarily give them any causal efficacy. In this sense supervenience is compatible with a diversity of positions, from the interactive dualism of Popper and Eccles to panpsychism (the belief that some form of consciousness exists throughout the system of nature), as well as nonreductive physicalism. By itself the notion of supervenience does not address the central issue of mental causation.

A sufficiently strong doctrine of top-down causation must go beyond simply describing the functioning of neural systems or finding correlations between conscious events of neuronal activity. A sufficiently strong doctrine of top-down causality must assert that supervenient properties now exert direct causal power over the lower levels, something Sperry does, in fact, assert very forcefully. However, if the higher-level properties can exert any kind of causality over their constituent parts, this implies that the larger system has causal properties not derived from or controlled by the causal properties of the parts. In this case, that the mind has causal powers not derived from the causal properties of the neurons.

There are at least two questions to be raised about any physicalist claim of downward causation. First, if these powers of causality are not entirely determined by the causal processes in the brain, where do they arise from? From where does the mind acquire the property of downward causation? It is certainly the case that the meaning of a word determines the order of the letters in that word, and that the function of a cell determines the behavior of the macromolecules that make it up. In that sense, they are exerting a kind of downward causality. Is this the same as the kind of downward causality the mind demonstrates in biofeedback and the placebo effect? A stronger example might be the ways in which a society regulates the behavior of its members. But this would require seeing the brain as a society of neurons in a very strong sense and not just as a convenient metaphor. For the analogy of brain and society to really work, the neurons would have to be given a certain degree of autonomy and agency, or perhaps the mind-brain is a strictly totalitarian state. That would just push the question down a level to the concern of where the individual neurons acquire this semi-autonomy. By escaping the Scylla of reductionism, nonreductive physicalism may veer close to the Charybdis of panpsychism.

Physical science has assumed the general features of a system are determined by the causal properties of its parts. The causal processes going on among its macromolecules govern what a cell can and cannot do. The meaning of the words govern what a sentence can and cannot mean. In most, if not all, theories of nonreductive physicalism, any causation at a higher level is derived from causation at a lower level. In none of these cases can the macro processes overrule or alter or even "structure" micro level causal activity. But in the case of consciousness, the nonreductive physicalist says that a new principle of causation, "top-down causation," suddenly appears and influences, if not overrules, the micro-level processes.

On the issue of consciousness as a cause, the nonreductive physicalist appears to be in a no-win situation. He can maintain the common scientific position that all causality arises from more fundamental lower-level processes, but then he would be practically indistinguishable from the reductive physicalist. And then mental causality becomes simply conjunction between neuronal and mental events. Thus mental causation is effectively denied, creating too weak a model of causation for mind-body medicine. Or he can affirm a strong causal power of consciousness to overrule, or at least redirect, those lower-level causal properties, but at the cost of leaving inexplicable the origin of this top-down causality.

And by claiming that a higher level of mental causality can act on lower-level processes in ways at least semi-independent

of that lower level's deterministic laws, he seems to be implying a violation of basic natural law. Of course, he might reply
that these higher-level causal powers are limited by the lower
level's properties, as the meaning of a sentence is limited by the
meanings of the words that make it up. But that is exactly what
a strong model of downward causation must deny. So either
downward causation must be weakened into insignificance or
basic natural laws must be violated.

The second concern is that if brain processes can be over-
ruled by a higher-order mental causation, as Sperry and others
suggest, then it would appear that the central nervous system
is not really a closed, physical system. But the principle of the
physical world as a closed system, not amenable to intrusions
from beyond, is a major assumption of scientific physicalism.
Of course, the nonreductive physicalist can assert that the mind
too is physical, operating within the constraints of the physical
world. But if you simply say that everything that is real is physical, and that consciousness is real, then consciousness becomes
physical by definition. A tautology is all that has been produced
here. Mental entities being real entails that mental entities are
physical, because real is equivalent to physical. The problem has
been solved by definition.

But a new problem has been created. What exactly is meant by
physical? What are the limits of the physical in the nonreductive
physicalist account? It would seem that the domain of the physical is without clear boundaries here. There seem to be no clear
criteria for what is genuinely, authentically physical. The reductionist says simply that the physical is what is described by the
physical sciences. Period. Here the reductive physicalist has the
virtue of simplicity. The nonreductive physicalist, on the other
hand, needs to assert that mental properties cannot be completely described in terms of physics and chemistry. Otherwise

they would be reductive physicalists. Yet they also want to say that mental properties are physical? But in what sense?

Once again, on the issue of consciousness as a cause, the non-reductive physicalist appears to be in a no-win situation. She can insist that mental processes are really physical and so the closure of the system of nature is not violated. But that claim may undercut any real difference between reductive and nonreductive physicalism. Or she can stress the difference between mental and neuronal domains, and so maintain her nonreductive stance. But then the sense in which her position is really physicalist is less clear.

These considerations leave me wondering whether nonreductive physicalism is really a coherent position. I'm not sure the nonreductive physicalist can have it both ways: trying to maintain both the reductive physicalist's tie to current natural science and the dualist's affirmation of conscious causality, without either vicious reductionism or scientific incompatibility.

In addition, it is clearly one thing to simply assert the arising of consciousness from neuronal activity; and it is something else to specify the actual processes by which that happens. Virtually all writers agree that no such account is currently available (for example, Libet, Chalmers, McGinn, Velmans). Some go as far as to suggest that we cannot even conceive of what such a count might hypothetically look like. All attempts to do that based in contemporary science have serious problems. Quantum theories have trouble finding places in which quantum events immediately appear in the ordinary world of brains and choices. Theories drawing on nonlinear dynamics and the emergence of complexity have trouble locating such processes in ordinary neurophysiology. Contrary to both quantum indeterminacy and chaos theory, the neurons in the brains seem to obey deterministic biological laws. And more to the point, advocates of quantum theories or nonlinear dynamics agree that such processes by themselves probably could not give rise to a strong version of downward causation (Silberstein, Scott). I do not want to push this point too hard. It is, after all, something of an argument from silence. The future may well produce a compelling scientific model of how neuronal processes give rise to conscious experience. But it should, at least, suggest a more humble and nuanced position than a simple assertion that consciousness is simply produced by the brain. And it also suggests that no current model of nonreductive physicalism can provide a sufficiently robust account of mental or downward causation. It appears that some additional factor must be added to our accounts of nature if they are going to explain the full range of conscious experience.

Incompleteness in Neuroscience

I have argued throughout this book that as a matter of logic, no scientific theory can or will ever be complete. It is not a criticism of any scientific model to say that it is not a complete account, for all theories are incomplete. There is perhaps another level of incompleteness here. There is a paradox in neuroscience: the primary instrument for studying the mind-brain is the mind-brain. Does that make neuroscience different from, say, physics or chemistry? It would probably be misleading to say that physics consists of electrons studying electrons or chemistry consists of chemicals studying chemicals, but it is not misleading to say that neuroscience consists of the brain studying the brain. The study of consciousness may contain a limitation that can never be completely resolved, since we are using the brain to study the brain and using the categories of cognitive processing to study the categories of cognitive processing.

Put another way, in our investigations of consciousness we never stand outside the domain of consciousness. Even the latest and most sophisticated brain-scanning technologies still take place within the field of consciousness. Only a conscious and intentional agent can invent such machines, design experiments using them, gather the results and interpret the data. Consciousness is presupposed in every experiment. Consciousness is never studied entirely from the outside. Rather all experiments and model building take place within the field of consciousness. To what extent this paradoxical situation limits the scientific study of consciousness is a complex and contested question. But the impact of that paradox, and its potential to limit our theorizing here, should not be ignored.

Another concern is the way in which our theoretical assumptions limit what we can affirm. One example, mentioned above, is the doctrine of the universe as a closed system. Might we consider nuancing, or even rejecting that belief? The idea of the universe's causal closure can be understood as an operating principle of natural science without having to claim it is the final and complete description of the universe. From a pragmatic perspective, such postulates as the causal closure of the physical world can be seen as heuristic instruments, not as inviolable natural "laws." For purposes of scientific investigation, the natural world is framed as a closed causal system. Part of the motivation of science is to see how much heuristic gain can be obtained from investigating the world on that assumption. It is obviously a lot. But the explanatory successes of science may have blinded us to the inherent limitations of all human systems of knowledge and may have led us to regard such principles as the causal closure of nature as absolute truths, rather than as exceedingly fruitful heuristic tools. If nonreductive physicalists could loosen the grip of the principle of causal closure on their thinking, they might be able to fashion a more coherent position.

Science itself may be pointing further in that direction with new disciplines like "quantum biology," where it appears that indeterminate quantum processes do affect ordinary physical processes like gene expression. And physicists recently demonstrated quantum effects in a macroscopic structure: an event which *Science* magazine called the most important scientific discovery of 2010 (reported on ScienceDaily.com, December 17, 2010). All of this suggests a previously unsuspected openness in ordinary physical matter. To the extent this proves true, it will have profound implications for our understanding of conscious agency and maybe even the possibility of a more transcendental agency similar to that affirmed in many religions.

What are the implications of these different types of incompleteness for the model of nonreductive physicalism? As we have seen, the need to be in continuity with the worldview of mainstream science has created serious problems for nonreductive physicalism, especially because of mainstream science's commitment to the causal closure of the physical world. Put bluntly, the standing incompleteness, in the senses previously discussed, within all current and I think future neurological theories, leaves room for multiple models of consciousness. No neurological account of the human person can be used to preclude all theological ones.

The problems with physicalism as a worldview and the inherent incompleteness in all frames of reference suggest that physicalism is probably not a complete or compelling account of the natural world, let alone of all that is really real. This suggestion opens up a space for enlarging our understanding of the natural world beyond that provided by reductive, and even nonreductive, physicalism. So, one response to the inability of physicalism to account for many of the attributes of humanity that both nonreligious humanism and more traditional religious viewpoints affirm would be to enlarge our understanding of the natural world so as to be able to include those human attributes within it.

Of course, this move is anathema to the debunkers of religion who have been the subject of this book so far. Most of them have only sarcasm for any significantly expanded vision of the nature of the physical world. Their whole polemic against religion depends on a very narrow, perhaps indefensibly narrow, model of the natural world. On the other hand, a move to expand our understanding of nature is made by many religious and humanistic thinkers who accept the mainstream interpretations of contemporary neuroscience and seek to locate a place for religious claims and humanistic concerns within them. What might that look like?

An Expanded, Religious Naturalism

The stark truth seems to be that natural science as currently conceived, the science that the cognitive science of religion takes as its foundation and that is the basis of its claims about religion, cannot provide a robust enough account of mental causation to account for the findings of research in behavioral medicine, meditation, hypnosis, and other fields of psychophysiology. Others have reached this same conclusion. For example, Kihlstrom and Velmans, and others who find even nonreductive physicalism wanting on logical grounds. If self-regulation research continues to be borne out, and I see no indications in the literature that it will not be, we may well have to revise our scientific consensus. We may be at one of those historical points where scientific research is uncovering data that cannot be adequately explained in terms of the reigning consensus of what is "scientific." This might serve as a warning to those engaged in the science-religion discussion not to base all their theorizing on any model of physicalism that may be empirically fraying at the edges.

This suggests that if consciousness and mental causation are going to be understood as part of the order of nature, a further expansion of our understanding of nature is in order. Put another way, if we are going to understand how consciousness emerges within nature, we may have to give nature powers or dimensions that go beyond any possible brand of physicalism. But this is possible only if we realize that physicalism is one limited and very incomplete description of nature. There may well be more realities that are "natural" than can be disclosed through a purely physicalist frame of reference. This is certainly the position of those who argue that only an expansion of what constitutes the boundaries of "the natural" can solve the problem of mental causation; for example "panpsychists," like David Griffin, for whom there must be a protoconsciousness distributed through the material world. Or those, like Chalmers, Velmans, and perhaps Nagel, who want to say that consciousness is another irreducible dimension of the universe. They are not required to theorize how consciousness came into nature but only that it is a necessary element of the universe as we know it, perhaps on analogy to the constants of fundamental physics. This is not necessarily a religious move. Many who argue for it are atheists. But it certainly expands the notion of the "natural." If mind or consciousness is inevitably a part of nature, that certainly pushes naturalism in a more religious, but not necessarily theistic, direction. A conscious ground to nature moves naturalism closer to certain Vedantic schools of Hinduism. And it also maps nicely onto the Neo-Platonic vision which played a central role in the development of several versions of Judaism, Christianity, and Islam and has clear resonances with other forms of Hinduism and Buddhism. Some religious scholars see the image of a conscious mind suffusing nature as the perennial core of all religious philosophies. One does not have to go that far to recognize that such a vision of mind as a necessary part of nature resonates with many religious viewpoints and would move naturalism in a less antireligious direction.

Beyond that, if reductive and nonreductive physicalism are neither complete or compelling accounts of nature, other versions of naturalism are possible; many of which have a more distinctly religious flavor and can properly be called "religious naturalisms." Such religious naturalism comes in many varieties, but all insist that nature has sacred, awe inspiring dimensions and that it exhibits, at least in *homo sapiens*, the capacity for self-transcendence. And they are united in their rejection of any robustly transcendental, "supernatural," agents.

In a book explicitly referring to itself as a work of religious naturalism, called *The Sacred Depths of Nature*, Ursula Goodenough explains various natural processes and then movingly and colorfully describes the religious emotions that they invoke in her. On this view, religious naturalism is primarily an affective response to the mystery, complexity, and power of nature. "What we are calling religious naturalism can yield deep and abiding spiritual experiences," she writes. The "religious" element here adds emotional resonance and a feeling for the sacred, awe and reverence to our encounter with the natural world, but not much additional understanding of nature beyond what science currently supplies. Such "deep and abiding spiritual experiences" are not "noetic," in William James's words; they are only "wondrous mental phenomena"; they provide little or no additional information about the world. Goodenough concludes

> And so I profess my faith. For me, the existence of all this complexity and awareness and intent and beauty, and my ability to apprehend it, serves as the ultimate meaning and the ultimate value. The continuation of life reaches around,

grabs its own tail, and forms a sacred circle that requires no further justification, no creator, no superordinate meaning of meaning, no purpose other than that the continuation continue until the sun collapses or the final meteor collides.

While profoundly moving, there is little sense that these deeply personal responses to nature reveal anything more about nature.

Wesley Wildman suggests that they do, stating that our religious-like reactions to nature imply something about nature too. He describes a religious naturalism which supplies additional ways of understanding, as well as relating to, nature.

> In a fully naturalistic framework ... there is not supernatural realm, no divine beings.... There is enormous richness of value in the structures and processes of nature, however, from heart-rending beauty to complexly ambiguous moral possibilities, and from glorious mathematical patterns to staggeringly counterintuitive physical transactions. These depths of nature have important existential implications and are subject to phenomenological, existential, philosophical, and theological renderings.... This kind of value-sensitive naturalism leads directly and easily to a religious naturalism.

The metaphor of depth runs throughout Wildman's book, for example, "reality has an axiological depth" and religious experiences "open up to us the value-laden depths of this world." Here religious naturalism embraces but goes beyond purely scientific or physicalist models and points to sources of value and meaning intrinsic in nature that science alone leaves out.

Robert Corrington writes of what he calls "ecstatic naturalism," which begins from the human drive for understanding. This very human desire for understanding is rooted in "the natural and spiritual potencies that give shape to meaning and communication." Corrington often speaks of the power of the spirit, but the spirit he refers to is enfolded within nature, since "at the heart of nature is the power of the spirit that enlivens and directs our interpretative life." Unlike Wildman, Corrington is more than willing to use the term "God." But the God of his text is a God completely embedded in nature: "God is manifest in the depths of nature and the psyche, and speaks through the sacramental potencies of nature." Thus God is the dynamism within the natural world. "God, while not a person or a self, lives as the energy that makes selving [becoming a self] and individuation possible." Ecstatic naturalism is far from a reductive naturalism. Rather this is a God-imbued naturalism "that honors the self-transcending potencies within nature which continually renew the orders of the world."

Further along what appears to be a continuum, from the emotion-evoking but basically scientific naturalism of Goodenough to the self-consciously religious naturalism of someone like Wildman, to something like the naturalism of the transcendentalists as articulated by someone like Corrington, is the theistically infused naturalism of Holmes Rolston. In a book that provides a clear and comprehensive review of recent developments in epistemology, physics, biology, and other scientific domains, Rolston argues with detailed examples that current scientific findings not only evoke awe and mystery but also open up nature to overtly theological interpretations. Conceiving of the physical world in quasi-theological as well as scientific metaphors is now possible for Rolston because contemporary science models a more complex and open-textured universe than during the highpoint of Newtonian mechanics. Rolston writes

The nature we do know has grown soft. There is something hazy that we can touch with our formulas but hardly imagine. There is a subsurface inaccessibility, plasticity, and mysteriousness that allows us more easily to be more religious now than in the hardworld of earlier physics. The old themes of materialism—atomic matter in absolute motion, sensory and pictorial substance, total specifiability, mechanics, predictability, finished logical analysis—have every one an antithesis in recent physics. It is hard to know what synthesis to make, but certainly a religious synthesis is not precluded. Nature is now less material, less absolutely spatiotemporal, more astounding, more open, an energetic developmental process. . . . If in one sense this nature is still secular, in another sense it is a suitable arena for the operation of a sacred, creative Spirit.

Rolston calls this position "transscientific theism," in which "Nature is a sacrament of the divine presence, and remains so after the best descriptions of science have been received. Nothing known in science prevents the divine superintending of natural processes. To the contrary . . . science finds an open-ended nature that is a fitting field for the divine providence." Rolston is even willing to rehabilitate the term "supernatural" when he writes "To believe in the supernatural is to take the epiphenomena seriously. . . . *Life* does appear, afterward *mind*, but are these (as hard naturalism maintains) nothing but epiphenomena. . . . A further supernatural power would not be any more or less miraculous than what has already taken place under so-called natural powers. . . . To believe in the supernatural is to insist on keeping the concept of the natural open-ended, to refuse to close the system." And Rolston quotes the concluding sentences of the evolutionary paleontologist Loren Eiseley's 1946 book, *The Immense Journey*,

I would say that if "dead" matter has reared up this curious landscape of fiddling crickets, song sparrows, and wondering men, it must be plain to even the most devoted materialist that the matter of which he speaks contains amazing, if not dreadful, powers and may not impossibly be, as Hardy has suggested, "but one mask of many worn by the Great Face behind."

Here religious naturalism shades off into a transcendental theism with a robust doctrine of divine immanence. The history of theology in the Abrahamic traditions reveals numerous differing and complex ways of relating God's transcendence to God's immanence in the world. Reviewing these differing theologies is far, far beyond the scope of this book. But such a history would illustrate that there is no necessary or inevitable cognitive dissonance between affirming a spiritual or sacred presence in the depths of nature and also affirming a divine reality that transcends nature by giving rise to it and encompassing it. One example: early Jewish and Christian thinkers like Philo and Origen made the Stoic concept of the "logos" (the Greek word from which we get our term "logic), which referred to the deep structures of the physical world, into an attribute of God. Thus they affirmed a divine presence throughout the cosmic system. But that is beyond the bounds of what is usually described as religious naturalism. From the standpoint of such a transcendental theism, religious naturalism is correct in what it affirms about nature but wrong in what it denies, when it denies any transcendental sacred reality.

This is a very cursory review of the history of a certain strand of religious thought. Obviously none of these positions are developed in anywhere near the depth or subtlety they deserve. Religious naturalism is naturalistic but eschews a simplistic physicalism; and it affirms a spiritual dimension to reality while remaining naturalistic in some sense. Of course the debunkers find any moves beyond reductive physicalism and classical Darwinism to be fantasy and wishful thinking. Freud said the same thing. But this brief discussion shows that there is a wide spectrum of positions between a narrow and reductive physicalism and the belief in supernatural agents and immortal souls, which the debunkers take as the defining characteristics of religion. None of these versions of religious naturalism believe in outright supernatural agency or immortal souls. None of the debunkers' arguments from cognitive science would tell against them. Yet they are clearly understood by their devotees to be religious in some sense. This may just underscore the narrowness of the debunkers' understanding of religion.

The more we expand our definition of nature, the more the cognitive science of religion loses its debunking edge. Whether that is good or bad depends on the assumptions and sensibilities we bring to the discussion. But clearly the claim that religion is natural would have very different implications if it were argued from within one of these expanded views of nature as opposed to a reductive physicalism. If nature itself has sacred depths or is spirit-infused or even God-infused, and has consciousness and intentionality as part of its most fundamental structures, then the fact that natural processes give rise to religion could be interpreted as telling us something about nature as well as something about religion. Yes, religion is natural but then nature is also religious. An expanded definition of nature provides us with an expanded cognitive science of religion, in which the investigation into the natural origin of religion can be construed as also an investigation into the deeper religious origin of religion.

I have argued in this chapter that the study of consciousness cannot be contained in a narrowly physicalist framework and that it requires a broadening of our understanding of physical reality beyond reductive physicalism. The study of consciousness may drive us to make additional claims beyond physicalism about physical reality and about the connection of consciousness itself to nature, that is, about nature's consciousness-generating powers. Even more radically, the cognitive science of religion may lead us to make further claims about nature, that is, about its sacred depths and its religion-generating powers. Rather than undermining a religious naturalism or even a transcendental theism with a strong immanentalist dimension, such a cognitive science of religion might offer them additional support.

Conclusion: The Place of Religion in the Discussion of Human Nature

The kind of physicalism that undergirds the antireligious arguments of the debunkers is simply not compelling or convincing, especially when it encounters the problems of conscious awareness and mental causation, a conclusion reached by many thinkers who are not religious and who may be overtly atheistic. I have argued that even the strongest versions of nonreductive physicalism are not robust enough to account for the kind of downward causation displayed in behavioral medicine and other domains of experience. Religious people, religious naturalists, Neo-Platonists, and transcendental theists have additional intellectual resources to address the problem of consciousness. That is one of my main assumptions. For example, religious people, for whom the system of nature is part of a larger and more encompassing reality, need not, and probably should not, absolutize the metaphor of nature as a causally closed system. In a more encompassing religious framework, proposed solutions to the problem of consciousness that make no sense in a more limited physicalist framework become coherent. For example, Chalmers and Velmans proposal that there is a more encompassing reality, which subsumes both consciousness and the physical world, makes sense in the context of those religious philosophies that have always affirmed that the physical world has a spiritual dimension or is the expression of a spiritually encompassing reality. If consciousness is a fundamental feature of nature, then there is little mystery about how it comes to emerge in the course of evolutionary development.

Or, meditative practices can train the practitioner to experience the ways in which consciousness gives rise to the thoughts and the categories through which we experience the world, including the scientific models we use to study consciousness. Such experiential knowing makes it harder to lose sight of the fact that, in all our studies of consciousness, we never escape the domain of consciousness. Consciousness is presupposed in every human method of understanding. It is the final basis of every claim we make. In that sense it pervades every object we know. In meditation this theoretical assertion is given experiential validation. In meditation we may become aware that central to mind or consciousness, as they are known experientially, is the activity of generating our awareness and the categories that shape that awareness. This insight, into the creative power of consciousness and its inseparability from everything we know, can be a window on a reality beyond that subject-object duality in which natural science and its offshoots in cognitive neuroscience are confined. Such, at least, is the testimony of generations of Buddhist and Christian contemplatives, as well as those from many other traditions.

Such traditions which might loosely be called "contemplative" claim that within the depths of human consciousness is a window on the universal and the divine. In all religions, such a claim is presented as a quasi-empirical one that can be demonstrated within experience by those willing to undertake the requisite spiritual disciplines. Those whose religious practice involves the immediate experience of an immanent divine source may demand a rather different understanding of human nature than that offered by even the most nonreductive physicalism. Or, to put it differently, even nonreductive physicalism, like all strict physicalisms, may provide too narrow a definition of human nature to explain or to support the full range and richness of religious practices and experiences. In addition, a model that combines reciprocal bottom-up and top-down causality complicates the rather simple, linear version of causality, in which cognitive science claims that religious beliefs are simply the result of cognitive mechanisms and neuronal firings.

Chapter 5

Our Pluralistic Universe

Living on the Border of Science and Religion

We have suggested that findings from cognitive science do not weaken or refute a religious outlook, since showing that we have such cognitive processes as agency detection and theories of mind, and claiming that religious beliefs arise from them, does not entail that these mechanisms are the only sources of religious belief, just as showing that we may have a causality-detection capability does not entail that it is the only source for the claims of natural science. There may be other factors that are sources for religious outlooks, and pointing to them will provide additional reasons for religious convictions. And understanding the process that leads a person to have a belief says nothing about the truth or falsity of the belief. The problems with the debunkers' use of cognitive science do not come from cognitive science per se, but primarily from interpreting its findings from a reductive physicalist framework. In that sense, my dispute with the debunkers is, in most cases, about their basic intuitions and the judgments that lead them to embrace that framework. I have also suggested that when the dispute involves intuitive cognitions and background assumptions, reasons can still be given for differing positions but they must be pragmatic reasons, not coercive proofs. This leads naturally to other ways of relating religion and science besides using science to debunk religion.

Giving Reasons for Basic Beliefs

The religious person, whether they are a religiously inclined nonreductive physicalist, a devotee of religious naturalism, or a believer in transcendental theism, can certainly give pragmatic reasons for their basic sensibilities and chosen frames of reference. Such assumptions are not just intuitively appealing, although that is true for a religious person, but the religious person can certainly and correctly claim that these assumptions make sense of their daily experiences. Of course there is a circularity in this. The experiences they pay attention to and take seriously are shaped and governed by their religious schemas. Just as the basic sense that causality operates in the physical world is confirmed by our regular reliance on it to find our way around the ordinary world, so our religious sensibilities can help us find our way around the moral world. And, if we choose to engage in it, they can help us find our way around the spiritual world, the world of prayer, worship, service, and the love of wisdom. Such pragmatic reasoning does not prove but rather supports a religious outlook.

So if a person wanted to give reasons for the sensibility that undergirds their religious convictions, they should offer pragmatic considerations. They should describe what their religious convictions do. They might, for example, say that religion helps them make sense of their experiences in the world. Both science and religion claim to do that. That is a similarity between science and religion: at a very general level they both help us make sense of our experiences in the world. But the types of experience they each focus on are very different. That is a difference between science and religion. Religion is not about making sense of laboratory experiences or statistical analyses. What sort of experiences might religion be called upon to help us understand? There are several possible candidates, most of which are central to both religious naturalism and theism. This is a short and very incomplete list of possibilities:

(1) What might be called "gestalt" experiences, from the German world *Gestalt*, which means "whole" or refers to an "integrated unity," combining different facets of experience. These are experiences of unity, wholeness, coherence, when things seem to just "fall into place," or when we become aware of our unity with nature or with humanity.

(2) "Boundary experiences" that push us to the limits of our ordinary, taken-for-granted sensibilities: suffering, unexpected coincidence, great joy, miracle, death. Here we may be forced to the limits of our ordinary understandings and so be catalyzed to possibly see beyond them to a greater reality.

(3) Mystical experiences that might bring an apparently immediate sense of an encompassing, spiritual presence. Such experiences are often the result of disciplined practices. William James, for example, argues that such experiences are "noetic," that is, they provide us with knowledge of ourselves and our place in the world that is not available in any other way.

(4) Awe in the face of nature: the beauty of the sunset, the awesomeness of a great mountain range, the complexity of cells, the symmetries of fundamental physical interactions, the "fine tuning" of the universe.

(5) The call of moral duty, as exemplified in the lives of a Gandhi or a Martin Luther King Jr., and the saints and

moral exemplars of the world's religions, when the sense of moral obligation reforms a person's life. This involves two interrelated but separate concerns: the derivation of moral values and generating the motivation to act on them. I have already suggested that generating moral values from empirical descriptions alone probably has insuperable logical problems. Beyond that, even if moral values could be derived empirically, such a logical demonstration may have little success in actually motivating people to act morally. We have known for decades that an environmental crisis looms, but appeals to self-interest or empirical facts did not generate much concern. There is a reason that major moral movements like the anti-slavery movement in England and America or the civil rights movement in America were mainly led by the religiously motivated.

(6) Accounts of historical events: the exodus from Egypt; the life, death, resurrection of Jesus; the call of Mohammed; the awakening of the Buddha.

Not all of these will be equally compelling to everyone, and there are some, like die-hard physicalists, for whom none will be compelling in a religious sense. But these are examples of the types of common, widespread experiences that people often call on religious ideas to help them make sense of. And it is not illogical of them to do so. Also, while reductive physicalist accounts are possible of all of them taken separately, the limits and problems with relying solely on purely physicalist explanations has been the subject of this book. So such explanations do not necessarily vitiate the power of experiences like these. More importantly, for the religious person the various elements in a life of religious practice interact together and sum up into a reality that is experienced as more than just the parts seen separately. And that is a reasonable way, in keeping with current scientific models, to understand the religious life.

So one set of practical reasons that religious people might use to support their primary sensibility, is the help religious ideas provide in making sense of those experiences that seem to them to point beyond themselves to another dimension or domain of reality. But there are other functions that religious sensibilities also might perform. Again this is hardly a complete list:

(1) To give meaning to life and to death by locating one's life in a larger, transcendental context. Psychological research finds that religion is a potent, perhaps the most potent, source for a sense of meaning in life. Research also finds that having a sense of meaning is a powerful contributor to human flourishing.

(2) To be a source of moral guidance for the religious person; obviously nonreligious people find other sources of moral guidance.

(3) To answer questions about the ultimate origin and destiny of the universe, and of its fundamental properties, and of human existence within it.

(4) To support the sense that human personhood is valuable, even sacred.

(5) To open access to a power and reality that transcends the ordinary world, and to create an ethos of appreciation of that transcendental power through worship, contemplative, and devotional practices.

These are obviously not the kinds of concerns one answers by designing an experiment or performing a mathematical analysis. One must look elsewhere to find places where these tasks are carried on and these questions are explored and answered. To the extent that a person is open to these concerns and that religious ideas and practices are successful in performing these functions for them, an intuitive religious sensibility will be compelling and reasonable. Reductive physicalism may provide, at least to the physicalist, possible reasons to dismiss such concerns. But the task of this book is to raise questions about the limits of those physicalist accounts. To the extent that one accepts that such accounts are limited, one might be open to the kinds of experiences and concerns listed here. Given that empirical accounts of such experiences and concerns, as well as skeptical arguments against them, are possible, I am not saying that the world is such that it demands a religious response. Rather, I would insist only that the world is ambiguous as regards the need for ultimate explanations and ultimate concerns; the world as we know it offers both grounds for religious convictions and reasons to be skeptical of them. That, along with the "underdetermination of theory by data," means that religious accounts and concerns are not irrational.

That is as much as I need to say. I hope I have been clear that my purpose in writing this book is not to defend religion, let alone to "prove" the truth of religious claims. My only purpose is to argue that those who seek to use cognitive science to disprove or debunk religion are going far, far beyond what the findings of cognitive science support or ever could support. So the reasons given here for holding a religious outlook on the world are in no way intended to "prove" the truth of such a religious outlook or to convince a skeptic. I have even suggested that attempting to "prove" the truth of religion or convince a skeptic is probably futile, since skeptical and religious convictions rely on a more tacit domain that is not amenable to proof or disproof. It is enough if I have shown that cognitive science does not undermine a religious perspective, even one that involves belief in a transcendental reality or a spiritual dimension of humanity, and that holding such a position is in no way irrational or antiscientific, and that religious people can offer perfectly rational reasons for believing as they do. To say otherwise is mistaken.

Reflective analysis, I hope like the kind offered in this book, can push both the religious devotee and the physicalist debunker to the limits of their conscious, explicit beliefs and so uncover the more tacit, implicit cognitions and sensibilities that drive them. At this point discussion does not have to cease or degenerate into rhetoric and polemic; especially if each can accept the inevitable incompleteness and limitations of their own perspectives. Deeper reasons can still be offered and debated. They will not be coercive demonstrations or universally valid proofs. They will more likely be pragmatic, functional reasons, the kind that can finally be known to be true only by commitment and living them out. However, such a discussion can produce a gain in mutual understanding, even when it fails to produce conversion to either a physicalist or a religious worldview.

Pluralism

As should be clear by now, a pluralistic sensibility is a corollary of my emphasis on pragmatism and on the inevitable incompleteness of all our explanations. Given different implicit starting points, different frames of reference, different things they focus on, and the different kinds of categories and methods they deploy, many different but correct explanations for the same phenomenon are possible, even inevitable. In this sense cognitive science and religious belief and practice do not conflict.

I have just been given a painting as a gift. Wanting to know its value, I ask for an analysis of the painting from an art historian, a professor of aesthetics, and a gallery owner. The art historian tells me where such a work would fit in the history of art.

The professor of aesthetics admires its balance, form, and subtle use of color. The gallery owner appraises its market value. A colleague from the chemistry department stops by in the midst of this discussion and tells me about the chemical composition of the various pigments.

We have several different accounts of the same painting. Each one is presumably correct, if carried out properly. But they do not conflict. The chemist's account of the nature of the pigments is true, but wildly incomplete. It tells us nothing about the aesthetics of the work, since many beautiful and many ugly paintings have the same chemical composition. The historian has properly traced the development of the artist's style but that tells us little about its monetary value; many works in that style are worthless on the market. So how do we decide which account to attend to? That goes back to the functional, pragmatic nature of explanations. What do we want our explanation to do? What questions do we want our explanation to answer? If we want to know why the painting is worth $100,000, we ask the gallery owner and not the chemist. If we want to know why it has faded over time, we ask the chemist and not the aesthetics professor. And so on.

The reasons we give and the explanations we offer are a function of the goals we want to accomplish. And since human beings are very complex, as a species we have many different goals we want to accomplish and different kinds of questions we want to explore. If I want to know why the shoreline in front of our home has the shape it does, I consult a text of geology, not a political history of the county. But if I want to know if that natural environment makes a moral claim on me for its protection, a geological textbook will do me no good. I had best consult a sacred text or the moral philosophy of a religious tradition. If I want to know about the geometric structure of the universe, I do not engage in a meditative practice but rather learn some mathematical physics. But if I want to investigate the ultimate origin of the symmetries and conservation laws on which physics depends, a religious perspective will be needed. If I want to understand the motivations behind performing a liturgy or sitting in meditation, a psychological analysis can provide that. If I want to know if liturgy and meditation can transform my view of the world and my ethical stance, the psychological analysis will be of little use. The psychology of religious experience is no substitute for religious experience.

Compartmentalization versus Conflict

A corollary of this pragmatic and contextually oriented approach to the relationship between science and religion is a certain degree of compartmentalization. This is reminiscent of the evolutionary biologist Stephen Jay Gould's often-repeated suggestion that religion and science be seen as "non-overlapping magisteria" (universally abbreviated as NOMA), that is completely and totally separate in every way. My problem with Gould is not his compartmentalization—which I basically accept, in a less extreme form—but rather with how he divides up the two domains. Religion, in his view, can say absolutely nothing about the physical world or even our ordinary experiences, but is confined to moral values and ultimate questions.

Richard Dawkins replies to Gould that religion does make claims about the physical world and everyday life and therefore does conflict with science. From a pluralistic position, my question to both Gould and Dawkins is about whether all statements about the physical world are necessarily scientific in a strict sense. My example of the painting would suggest otherwise. The historical, the philosophical, even the monetary analyses are rational, but not scientific in the experimental sense. Yet they are still about the painting. Discussions about the "fine tuning" of the universe or whether random mutation and chance variation alone, when combined with natural selection, provide a complete account of speciation are clearly about the world. Still, they go beyond scientific data, since both sides refer to the same data while interpreting it very differently. So I agree with Dawkins against Gould that religion can make statements about the physical world. But I would insist that there may be important and valid statements about the physical world that are not strictly scientific. Put another way, the compartmentalization I am suggesting concerns differing interpretations of similar data and experience; it does not have to refer to totally different domains, as Gould's "non-overlapping magisteria" would demand.

Religion and science can directly conflict only if either (1) You are committed to an epistemological zero-sum game, in which there is only one, single valid way to see the world, or (2) you think that religion and science perform exactly the same functions, answer the same kinds of questions, aim at solving exactly the same types of problems. While the arguments presented in this book provide reasons why neither of these alternatives need be compelling, there clearly are people involved in apparent disputes between science and religion who hold firmly to one or both of those alternatives. I would say they are involved in disputes rather than discussions or dialogues precisely because they are committed to one or both of those alternatives.

There are clearly religious people and self-appointed spokespersons for science who insist on an epistemological zero-sum game and that there can be only one valid way to see the world, like Dennett's positivism which insists that "there is no better source of truth on any topic than well-conducted science." Obviously my advocacy of pluralism, my insistence on the necessary incompleteness of all worldviews and systems of explanation, my reliance on pragmatism as the court of last resort, all serve to undercut such a narrow epistemology. In addition, I would point to the complexity of human nature and to the variety of concerns and interests that have motivated hominids from the beginning of the species, as undermining any demand that all people should see the world entirely the same way and engage in the same practices. I think there are very strong reasons to adopt a pluralistic outlook, but I know that it does not appeal to everyone. And I will avoid putting on my psychoanalytic cap and offering an analysis of why that might be so. My point here is that if you really want to make religion and science conflict, you can easily do so by insisting on a singular worldview, either scientific or religious. But you do not have to.

On the current scene, we tend to call people who insist that their religion is the one and only truth "fundamentalists," not a term I find very helpful. As there are religious "fundamentalists," so there are scientific "fundamentalists," including some in the cognitive science camp. They need each other. Each provides the target for attack that the other demands. Each provides the straw person the other needs as evidence for their opposing position. They are dancing partners, perfectly in sync. Together they keep the dance of conflict going. A more pluralistic and multidimensional epistemology allows one to forsake that dance and move on. Here are four common, contested cases that illustrate how we might move beyond that dance of conflict.

A contested case: In order to try to refute religion by using science, one must deny pluralism and insist that religion and science are functional equivalents. McCauley comes close to this in his 2000 article contrasting the naturalness of religion with the unnaturalness of science; I think this is less true of his 2011 book. He realizes that comparing science and religion requires showing they perform the same function, otherwise they could not conflict or be compared. I find this claim particularly hard to maintain. If you start from a very generic definition of explanation you can appear to make it work, which is what I think McCauley does. You might say explanation means locating the phenomenon to be explained in a larger framework that makes sense of it. Newton located the phenomenon of falling bodies in a mathematical framework. Hinduism locates the question of human nature in a framework formed by Yogic practice, disciplined meditation, and Upanishadic philosophy. While obviously true, that basically descriptive claim about common explanatory functions does not really tell us a lot. It is much, much too general. The more important question concerns the functions performed for doing those things. Is Newton's mathematical formulation of falling bodies designed to perform the same kind of function as Yoga, meditation and thinking about the world using categories from the Upanishads? I think probably not. To call them both "explanations" is true in that they both serve to make sense of the phenomena under consideration. But that very generic notion of explanation confuses more than it enlightens.

Another contested case (if it is hard to follow don't worry, it is only an example): Physics today offers a fiercely mathematical account of the first few microseconds of the universe's existence, involving questions about how the most basic forces, symmetries, and constants (for example gravity, Planck's constant, etc.) might combine into the universe we know. One major unsolved problem, at the time of this writing, involves unifying General Relativity, which deals with large objects like planets and galaxies, and Quantum Mechanics, which deals with the smallest and most fundamental constituents of matter. One goal of research in contemporary physics is to construct a mathematical model harmonizing these two theories. Now I think it is intuitively obvious that when the Hebrew scriptures declared that "God created the heavens and the earth," they were not seeking to unify General Relativity and Quantum Mechanics. They were not seeking to provide a mathematical model of the universe. They were affirming that the universe, whatever its physical and mathematical constitution, is dependent on a source beyond itself. They were not doing primitive physics. They were not doing physics at all. Only if I think that the Hebrew scriptures' declaration of God's creativity or the Tibetan teaching about the cycles of the many worlds were designed to answer the questions that plague mathematical physicists today, or that the complex mathematical formulae of contemporary cosmology were designed to affirm the transcendental grounding of the universe—that is, only if I think they are performing the same function—can I logically say that religion and science can conflict here.

Yet another contested case: If I read the book of Genesis as though it were a biology textbook, seeking to answer questions about the biological drivers of the process of speciation or to deny that there is a process of speciation, then I have created a conflict between religion and science. But to read it that way, I have to think that the authors of the Hebrew scriptures had in mind questions about the heritability of populations and the relationship of genotypes and phenotypes. Not likely! I don't think they were seeking to answer the kinds of questions current biological theory struggles with. Rather, I think they might have had in mind issues of moral responsibility ("the knowledge of good and evil") as being central to the human condition. Biological theory and the book of Genesis address different questions. Their accounts perform radically different functions. There is no necessary conflict here.

The most serious case of this confusion of religion and science occurs in the widespread claim that religion is a primitive form of science. When I was beginning to study and later to teach religious studies and I encountered that statement, I put it down to ignorance on the part of people who had not studied these things. Having not studied religion, they did not understand what our ancestors' religious statements, "myths" if you wish, were really doing. Even then, I could not believe that people really thought that ancient Greek stories about gods pushing the sun through the sky were actually addressing the same concerns as Einstein's General Theory of Relativity. But now I am older and grumpier and much more suspicious, and I suspect that claim about religion being primitive science is kept alive for more nefarious reasons: to enable people who should know better to insist that since religion is but primitive science, it can and should be replaced by physics, chemistry, biology, or cognitive neuroscience. That insistence is reasonable only on the mistaken view that they perform equivalent functions.

So I reject the common cliché that scientific "explanations" are replacing religious "explanations." They are doing no such thing. The word "explanation" is being used in radically different senses in these two references. Religions never were offering "explanations" on the model of natural science. I don't know any sacred text of any world religion that uses the word "explanation" or uses a similar term with a science-like meaning. Rather, in the case of the Hebrew scriptures, they are making a claim about the ultimate source of time and space and about humanity's inherently moral nature.

So like Dawkins, I agree that religions do make claims about the world; both religious naturalism and transcendental theism certainly do. But because the claims of religion perform completely different functions than the claims of physics or biology, like the claims of the chemist and the art historian regarding the painting, there can be statements about the world that are not scientific and therefore not in conflict with science. Affirming that the universe has deeper, sacred dimensions or processes at work, or is sourced by a power outside itself, or that moral responsibility is central to what it means to be human is not to propose scientific theories. Such statements are about the world, but they will not be verified by experiment or mathematics. They will be verified only by commitment and practice.

Conclusion

In the *God Delusion* Dawkins argues that in earlier times religion had a certain degree of credibility, but the coming of natural science has made religious commitment totally irrational. This book has not sought to defend any particular religion or religion in general, but simply to argue that Dawkins is wrong there. Natural science, even the cognitive science of religion, does not render irrational the choice to live life in a religious mode. The reasons given against such a choice are not coercively convincing or particularly compelling; and perfectly good reasons can be offered in favor of such a choice.

A pluralistic approach makes possible living comfortably with a variety of approaches to understanding a life of religious practice, including those understandings born of both cognitive science and religious commitment. Only if we insist that there is just one valid way to understand religion or that religion and science fulfill the same functions, answer identical questions, and utilize the same methods, can we reasonably say they must conflict and contradict. If we recognize that as human beings we have a variety of types of questions we want answered, problems we want solved, and issues we want to understand, we can happily live within a pluralistic universe.

Cognitive science provides interesting insights into the possible cognitive underpinnings of religious belief—our propensity to look for teleology and agency, the presence of constraints on our cognition, the way that some ideas are easier to remember and so remain in circulation—and suggestions for additional lines of research. That is all to the good. If the cognitive psychology of religion remained there, there would be no need for a book like this. There is nothing here that explains religion in its entirety or undermines or debunks it. But those whom I call the debunkers go far, far beyond these claims. In a remarkable stretch of interpretative overreach, they assert that they have indeed "explained" religion, broken its spell, demonstrated its falsity, even its pathology, and left the religiously inclined "with their tongues hanging out, dying for a drop of faith." Rarely, if ever, in science or philosophy has the conclusion so far exceeded the argument.

Sources, References,
and Further Discussions

Since this book is written for general readers I have not laden the text with footnotes or references. Here I provide references where research and arguments supporting what I say can be found. Some of the topics are so broad or so contested that even in this appendix, I can provide only very limited references. To do otherwise would be to write another book or several books.

Introduction

These statements by Jesse Bering were reported in Murray (2009, p. 169). The statements by Daniel Dennett can be found in Dennett (2006, p. 217).

Cognitive science has so far concentrated on three sets of beliefs: in "supernatural agents," in a nonphysical part of human nature ("souls") and other disembodied entities (ghosts, spirits, ancestors, etc.), and in a sense of the world as displaying "purpose" or "teleology." In this book I am following cognitive science and am not being drawn into a larger debate over definitions of religion, since that is not my focus here. I have abstracted these beliefs a bit into claims about a "reality beyond the physical world" and a "spiritual dimension" to human nature, in order to relate these claims to more of the world's religions. Hindus and Buddhists do not necessarily believe in personal supernatural agents, although many adherents do; but they do believe there is more to reality than the material world and that human beings possess a "spiritual dimension." Buddhism is often brought up as a counter to claims about religion involving "supernatural beliefs," particularly by secular, North American Buddhists, and while it is true that the Buddha probably did not believe in a single, supernatural agent, the Buddha was certainly no Logical Positivist or reductive materialist. I develop this more in Jones (2003a).

Examples of my application of clinical, post-Freudian psychological models to religion and my response to the accusation of reduction can be found in *Terror and Transformation: The Ambiguity of Religion in Psychoanalytic Perspective* (London and New York: Routledge, 2002); *Religion and Psychology in Transition: Psychoanalysis, Feminism and Theology* (New Haven, CT: Yale University Press, 1996); *Transforming Psychoanalysis: Feminism and Religion*, ed. James W. Jones and Naomi R. Goldenberg, *Pastoral Psychology*, 40, no. 6 (1992); and *Contemporary Psychoanalysis and Religion: Transference and Transcendence* (New Haven, CT: Yale University Press, 1991).

The quote from Wilfred Sellers is from *Science, Perception and Reality* (London: Routledge, 1963), 173, Crane and Mellor (1990).

Chapter 1: Explanations

The material reviewed here on cognitive science theories of religion (CSR) is taken from the following books and papers; many of which go over the same ground, so that almost all the material described in this chapter can be found in any one of them: Atran (2002), Barrett (2004), Bering (2006), Bloom (2005), Boyer (2001), Dennett (2006), Guthrie (1993), McCauley (2011).

Similar reviews can be found in I. Pyysiainen, *Supernatural Agents* (New York: Oxford University Press, 2009), and M. Rossano,

Supernatural Selection: How Religion Evolved (New York: Oxford University Press, 2010).

For an account of the debate over the explanatory power of the HADD hypothesis, see I. Pyysiainen, "The Cognitive Science of Religion," in Watts and Turner (2014, pp. 1–21).

One of the best brief discussions of this material can be found in Atran and Henrich (2010, pp. 1–13). My concerns about their model are voiced in the text.

For discussions of the modular model of the mind and the recent movement in cognitive science away from a radically modular model, see for example Fodor (2001) and Descombes (2001). Wildman (2011) also expresses skepticism about modular models. Carruthers (2006) claims to be arguing for modularity but, in fact, jettisons virtually all the characteristics of Fodor's and Pinker's massive modularity thesis, which still appears to dominate the popular cognitive science of religion discussion (J. Fodor, *The Modularity of the Mind* [Cambridge, MA: MIT Press, 1983], and S. Pinker, *How the Mind Works* [New York: Norton, 1997]). See reviews of Carruthers's book: Cowie (2008) and Machery (2008). An often referenced review by Barrett and Kurzban (2006) defends a revised and minimized modularity thesis, compared to the "early" form of Fodor and Pinker, and argues strongly for an interactionist model and against a direct, linear causal connection of genotype and neurophysiology including cognitive modules. This would appear to me to weaken the very strong evolutionary claims currently at work in much of the cognitive science of religion. Justin Barrett's most recent statements can be found in J. L. Barrett (2011), and in the response to N. F. Barrett's critical comments from which the quotations are taken (Barrett, 2010, p. 626). See also Turner (2014), for a critical review of the use of modular theory in CSR.

A report of some interesting experiments on the connections between affect and cognition in the domain of religious belief can be found in Thagard (2005).

On the issue of emergence and models of interactive systems, see for example Kaufman (1995), and I. Prigogine and I. Stengers,

Order Out of Chaos (New York: Bantam, 1984). For some of the theological implications of these models see R. J. Russell, N. Murphy, and A. R. Peacock (eds.), *Chaos and Complexity: Scientific Perspectives on Divine Action* (Berkeley, CA: Center for Theology and the Natural Sciences, 1997), and Clayton and Davies (2006). Extensive evidence and argumentation supporting the application of nonlinear dynamic models to neurology and cognition can be found in Freeman's research on olfactory sensation and other research reviewed in Gibbs (2005, chapter 3) and in Teske (2013).

Thus, part of the deeper, scientific background of my argument with certain approaches to cognitive psychology, has nothing to do with religion but rather with the empirical, clinical, and philosophical problems with these approaches' overemphasis on localization and modular models. This is obviously a controversy within cognitive neuroscience and their modular theories may prove better in the end, although the trajectory of the discussion does not appear to be going in that direction. But at least one can fairly say that the often unnuanced, literal reliance on such modular theories by some who write in the popular media about cognitive science and religion, is clearly not philosophically or scientifically defensible at this time.

Arguments that draw conclusions about our early ancestors' mental processes from research on contemporary children's cognitions seem to assume that the cognitive development of the species parallels individual cognitive development. This has often been referred to as "ontogeny recapitulates phylogeny." This thesis has been heavily criticized since the nineteenth century.

Chapter 2: Explaining

The discussion of the nature of explanation in this book reprises arguments that I have written about and deployed in religion-science discussions for over thirty years. They are developed in much more depth and detail in Jones (1981) and in a more popular mode written for the general public and undergraduate students in Jones (2006).

There is some difference of opinion within the CSR community about how central a role evolutionary theory should play in the explanation of religion. This controversy is discussed in Turner (2014). For example, Thagard (2005) argues strongly that evolutionary accounts provide little explanatory value in relation to religion.

On the issue of emergence and models of interactive systems, again see for example Kaufman (1995), and Prigogine and Stengers (1984). For some of the theological implications of these models see Russell, Murphy, and Peacock (1997), and Clayton and Davies (2006). Extensive evidence supporting the application of nonlinear dynamic models to neurology and cognition can be found in Freeman's research on olfactory sensation and other research reviewed in Gibbs (2005, chapter 3) and in Teske (2013). Oviedo (2008) also critiques Boyer and company for their overreliance on the modularity hypothesis (and provides an additional review of the critical literature), as well as for their oversimplification of religion as a loose collage of cognitive components. Likewise, Day (2004) provides an extensive critical commentary on the classical artificial intelligence (AI) and cognitive science models deployed in these writers' study of religion and argues that even the early religion of our ancestors was more cognitively complex than these theories can account for.

The quotation is from Clark and Barrett (2011, p. 655). Further arguments to support my insistence that an evolutionary account, or any account, of why a person comes to hold a belief entails nothing about the truth of that belief, see A. Visala, "The Evolution of Divine and Human Minds," in Watts and Turner (2014, chap. 4). The quotation from Mackie (1982) is on p. 197. The quotation from G. Kahane, "Evolutionary debunking arguments," *Nous*, 45, no. 1 (2011), 103–125, is on p. 105. See also R. White, "You Just Believe that Because . . . ," *Philosophical Perspectives*, 24 (2010), 573–615, and T. Bogardus, "The Problem of Contingency for Religious Belief," *Faith and Philosophy*, 30, no. 4 (2013), 371–392. My discussion of the issue of the justification of religious beliefs in the face of CSR is heavily reliant on the papers by Kahane, White, and Bogardus.

The classic studies of life-span cognitive development were done in the United States by James Fowler and his students, see J. Fowler, *Stages of Faith* (San Francisco, CA: HarperCollins, 1995), and in Europe by Fritz Oser; see F. Oser and P. Gmunder, *Religious Judgment: A Developmental Approach* (Birmingham, AL: Religious Education Press, 1991). This research has been updated by Heinz Streib: see H. Streib, R. W. Hood, B. Keller, R.-M. Csöff, and C. F. Silver, *Deconversion: Qualitative and Quantitative Results from Cross-Cultural Research in Germany and the United States of America* (Göttingen: Vandenhoeck & Ruprecht, 2009), and James M. Day: see J. M. Day, "Religion, Spirituality, and Positive Psychology in Adulthood," *Journal of Adult Development*, 17, no. 3 (published online December 9, 2009) and J. M. Day, 2008, "Human Development and the Model of Hierarchical Complexity: Learning from Research in the Psychology of Moral and Religious Development," *World Futures: The Journal of New Paradigm Research*, 64, nos 5–7 (2008), 452–467. Whether speaking of formal and postformal cognition, or hierarchical complexity, or integrative complexity, these studies agree that the most complex forms of reasoning and intelligence can be found among religious people at levels similar to or higher than the North American population at large. The insinuation that some of the debunkers make that religious people are less intelligent on average (for example by referring to themselves rather grandiosely as "the brights"—as opposed to what, the dull, the stupid?—that is, everyone else) is not borne out by any evidence. In a recent study, James M. Day, for example, found that the capacity for the most complex forms of reasoning were as common among the religiously devout as among atheists and agnostics; see J. M. Day et al., "Are Atheists More Enlightened than the Religiously Committed? Empirical Studies Using the Model of Hierarchical Complexity," a paper presented at the 2011 Congress of the International Association for the Psychology of Religion, Bari, Italy, August 2011. He told me his atheistic Harvard colleagues were shocked at first but they finally had to accept his evidence.

Boyer's suggestion that we can simply overlook more complex forms of religion is from Boyer (2003, p. 119). Day's claim about the complexity of even "primitive" religion is from Day (2007, p. 60).

The main quotes from McCauley (2011) are from pages 5, 7, 101, 104, 105, 117, 119, 147–148, 152–154, 211–214, 158, 159, 183, 213–214, 220, 221, 286, 321.

The quotation from E. O Wilson is from Clark and Barrett (2011, p. 663).

Others have critically covered this ground before me, especially Smith (2006 and 2010) and Robinson (2010). They are good books that certainly do a fine job of raising additional critical questions about the cognitive science of religion. Herrnstein Smith and Robinson are basically literary scholars. They do not deal as directly with the empirical foundations, or lack of them, of this (mis)use of CSR, nor with the more general epistemological issues that are on the boundary of science and religion. And they are associated with the "science studies" area, and most working scientists and related others I know are deeply suspicious of "science studies," for reasons I am not much in sympathy with. Dennett (2006) reflects this. From a more theological discussion, there are numerous books by Keith Ward, especially *Why There Almost Certainly is a God: Doubting Dawkins* (London: Lion Hudson, 2009). Similar arguments can also be found in Schloss and Murray (2009) and Watts and Turner (2014).

Descriptions of the theories of Müller, Tyler, and Fraser on the origin of religion can be found in D. Pals, *Eight Theories of Religion* (New York: Oxford University Press, 2006) and in I. Strenski, *Thinking about Religion* (Malden, MA: Blackwell, 2006).

The reference to Michael Polanyi is to *Personal Knowledge* (New York: Harper & Row, 1974).

Chapter 3: Physicalism

Many of the topics alluded to in this chapter—consciousness and the nature of the physical world—are mentioned only for purposes of illustration and are obviously not discussed in the depth and detail they deserve. Many have spawned hundreds of books and, in some cases, centuries of debate. Likewise, this list of references is also for illustration only and does not pretend to completeness. An adequate list of references for some of these topics would require a book.

On being able, or unable, to say clearly what the "physical" in physicalism refers too, see, for some relatively popular expositions, K. C. Cole, *The Hole in the Universe* (New York: Harcourt, 2001); P. Davies, *The Mind of God* (New York: Simon & Schuster, 1992). In more technical terms, see R. Feynman, R. Leighton, and M. Sands, *The Feynman Lectures on Physics* (Reading: Addison-Wesley, 1963), and J. D. Barrow, P. C. W. Davies, and C. L. Harper (eds.), *Science and Ultimate Reality: Quantum Theory, Cosmology and Complexity* (Cambridge: Cambridge University Press, 2004). I provide some historical background on these developments in relation to the science-religion discussion in Jones (1984).

I defend my claim that physicalism is not able to answer the question of consciousness in Jones (2003b and 1992). Much briefer versions of the same arguments can be found in chapter 4, below. See also D. Chalmers, *The Conscious Mind* (New York: Oxford University Press, 1996), Velmans (2000 and 1996), and Wallace (2012).

I review the research that suggests that human flourishing requires a sense of meaning and purpose in life in Jones (2004). See also H. Koenig, *Handbook of Religion and Health* (New York: Oxford University Press, 2001).

The quotation from Slingerland about being robots designed not to realize you are one is from 2008a, p. 281.

The quote from Quine is from Quine (1951, p. 41).

Quotations from Dennett (2006) are from pages 238–239.

I suggest here that in their polemic against religion, the debunkers are relying on a outmoded positivistic philosophy of science such as that represented by A. J. Ayer, whether they would refer to themselves as positivists or not, and that such a philosophy was decisively refuted by the leading mid-twentieth-century philosophers of science. See, for example, Toulman (1960), as well as:

Feyerabend, P. *Against Method*. New York: Verso, 1993.
Kuhn, T. *The Structure of Scientific Revolutions*. Chicago: University of Chicago Press, 1970.
Lakatos, I. *Philosophical Papers*, ed. J. Worrall & G. Currie. Cambridge: Cambridge University Press, 1978.

Lakatos, I., & Musgrave, A. *Criticism and the Growth of Knowledge*. Cambridge: Cambridge University Press, 1970.

Putnam, H. *The Many Faces of Realism*. LaSalle, IL: Open Court, 1987.

Toulmin, S. *Reason in Ethics*. Cambridge: Cambridge University Press, 1964.

Toulmin, S. *The Uses of Argument*. Cambridge: Cambridge University Press, 1958.

This decisive move away from Ayer's Logical Positivism is traced in J. O. Urmson, *Philosophical Analysis* (Oxford: Clarendon Press, 1956). I cover some of the same ground in Jones (1981). Much of this goes back to the foundational work of Wittgenstein in his later writings.

These references date from the latter half of the previous century. Have twenty-first-century philosophers of science gone back to something like the Logical Positivism of A. J. Ayer and his colleagues? Hardly. For current discussions of scientific explanation, see for example L. Sklar, "I'd Love to Be a Naturalist—If Only I Knew what Naturalism Was," *Philosophy of Science*, 77, no. 5 (2010), 1121–1137, and P. K. Stanford, "Damn the Consequences: Projective evidence and the Heterogeneity of Scientific Confirmation," *Philosophy of Science*, 78, no. 5 (2011), 887–899. Neither of these will provide much comfort to the positivists and narrow empiricists among the contemporary cognitive scientists studying, and attempting to debunk, religion.

The debunkers also claim that no rational arguments can be given to support a religious outlook. That is clearly false. A good introduction to the issue that overlaps with some of the concerns of this book is P. Clayton and S. Knapp, 2013, *The Predicament of Belief: Science, Philosophy, and Faith* (Oxford: Oxford University Press, 2013). In addition, see for example:

Alston, W. *Perceiving God*. Ithaca: Cornell University Press, 1991.

Hick, J. *Faith and Knowledge*. Ithaca: Cornell University Press, 1966.

Plantinga, A. *Warranted Christian Belief*. New York: Oxford University Press, 2000.

Swinburne, R. *The Existence of God.* Oxford: Clarendon Press, 1979.

Wainwright, W. *Reason and the Heart.* Ithaca: Cornell University Press, 1995.

Virtually all this discussion about the nature of science and warrants for religious beliefs in a scientific context is carried on in terms of Western religions, especially Christianity. For a discussion of some of these issues from a Buddhist perspective, see B. A. Wallace, *Contemplative Science: Where Buddhism and Neuroscience Converge* (New York: Columbia University Press, 2007) and Wallace (2012).

No one will find all of these different approaches convincing. A devoted physicalist will not find any convincing. But anyone who looks at these with a modicum of openness will be hard pressed to claim they are not rationally argued, using standard philosophical forms. My point is that the debunkers are wrong to imply that the relationship of science to the world is best understood in narrowly empricist terms and that no reasoned cases can be offered in support of a religious outlook. Since the goal of this book is not to argue for such an outlook, I will leave it there.

In contemporary biology the argument for an interactive relationship between genes, behavior, and the environment usually goes under the title of "epigenetics." An introduction can be found in J. Jablonka and M. Lamb, *Epigenetic Inheritance and Evolution: The Lamarckian Dimension* (Oxford: Oxford University Press, 1995), S. F. Gilbert and D. Epel, *Ecological Developmental Biology* (Sunderland, MA: Sinauer Associates, 2009), and also T. Grant-Downton and H Dickinson, "Epigenetics and its Implications for Plant Biology," parts 1 and 2, *Annals of Biology*, 95, no. 7 (2005), 1143–1164; 97, no. 1 (2006), 11–27. The example of the mice is from R. Waterland and R. Jirtle, "Transposable Elements," *Molecular and Cellular Biology*, 23, no. 15 (2003), 5293–5300.

For a further discussion of the tautological nature of the Darwinian theory of "natural selection," see Rolston (2006, pp. 95–105), from which the quotations are taken. Rolston cites several biological authorities who share this concern.

Material used in the discussion of our earliest ancestors can be found in *National Geographic* (2011, pp. 34–59); Fagen (2010); and Wilford (2012).

Justin Barrett (Clark & Barrett, 2011; Barrett, 2007; Barrett & Zahl, 2013) addresses some of the same concerns as this chapter, particularly as to whether naturalistic explanations make other accounts necessarily irrational or unconvincing, and argues at length for similar conclusions.

Additional critical discussion of the extent to which cognitive, evolutionary arguments can explain cultural phenomena like religion can be found in Watts and Turner (2014), especially chapter 11, L. Newson and P. Richerson, "Religion: The Dynamics of Cultural Adaptations," which argues for a "cognition-lite" model of culture, as opposed to the "cognition-heavy" model found in CSR. See also Laidlaw (2007).

Preston and Epley (2005) review three experiments that suggest that beliefs that can explain a range of phenomena are more valued than those whose accounts are more limited. Their experiments also suggest that some, rather minor, beliefs that can be explained by other beliefs do become less valued. Religious beliefs, among Harvard undergraduates, were tested, but only in terms of explaining God's hypothesized actions. Explaining belief in God itself was not tested. Their article hypothesizes that explanations of religious beliefs "may nevertheless seem to devalue religious beliefs," but even that rather weak claim was not tested. Nor was it tested in terms of other "highly valued" beliefs held by mature believers. There is, to my knowledge, at this time (2014) no experimental evidence that suggests that people will abandon religious beliefs simply because alternative explanations are offered. Of course the claim being made by the debunkers is not that people do that but rather that people *should* abandon their beliefs in the face of naturalistic explanations. But that injunction lacks force unless you are already predisposed to it.

Hawking discusses the concept of imaginary time in *A Brief History of Time* (New York: Bantam Books, 1988).

Weinberg writes that "the more the universe seems comprehensible, the more it also seems pointless." S. Weinberg, *The First Three Minutes* (New York: Basic Books, 1977), p. 154.

Chapter 4: Beyond Physicalism

Some of the arguments presented in chapter 4 are elaborated in more detail and with greater discussion of their implications for the religion-science field in Jones (2003b). In Jones (1992) I cover some of the same ground as here and I describe and analyze Sperry's position at length. I will not repeat that discussion here.

For a review of discussions on emergence, see the *Journal of Consciousness Studies*, 8, nos. 9–10 (2001) devoted to the topic, as well as Clayton and Davies (2006) and Tim Crane (2003b).

The position of nonreductive physicalism is taken from Brown, Murphy, and Maloney (1998). Quotations in the opening paragraphs are from Murphy (1998, p. 131), Sperry (1991, p. 244).

References for the hypnosis material are in Brown and Fromm (1987); Barber (1996); Rurzyla-Smith, Barabasz, Barabasz, and Warner (1995); Wood et al. (2003); Feldman (2004); and Sheikh, Kunzendorf, and Sheikh (1996).

References for biofeedback are in Basmajian (1983); Green and Green (1977); Schwartz and Beatty (1977); Kosslyn et al. (1993); Woody and Szechtman (2000); J. Schwartz (1999); and Goldapple et al. (2004).

References on meditation are in Marlatt and Kristeller (1999); Andresen (2000); Kabat-Zinn (1990); Shapiro, Schwartz, and Bonner (1998); Kristeller and Hallet (1999); Segal, Williams, and Teasdale (2002); Linehan (1993); Goleman (2003); and Davidson et al. (2003).

For more on problems with nonreductive physicalism, see Chalmers (1995), Velmans (2000), and H. M. Robinson (1976). Virtually all writers agree that no account of how the brain produces consciousness is currently available; see Libet (1982, 1996), Chalmers (1995), McGinn (1989), and Velmans (2000).

The positions of Clayton and Murphy are from Clayton (1999) and Murphy (1998, 1999a, 1999b). See also Meyering (1999) and Van Gulick (1993).

Philip Clayton (1999) maintains his position is not a form of physicalism, but he affirms a naturalistic monism. So if consciousness is not physical, it must be at least similar enough to what is physical to be part of the same system. Clayton does not specify what that similarity is. Sperry and Murphy both call their positions forms of physicalism.

This important question underlying much of this discussion regarding what constitutes a "property" or an "event" is exceedingly controversial in the philosophy of mind and is far beyond the scope of this book. See Heil and Mele (1993).

In many ways my argument here follows that of Kim (1998), where he repudiates his earlier advocacy of the position of nonreductive physicalism. And Kim is quite clear that he agrees that mental causation is inexplicable in a purely physicalist framework (Clayton & Davies, 2006, chapter 8). Clearly, however, I am using our common arguments in the service of a radically different position from Kim's. And I am arriving at it more from the standpoint of clinical and experimental evidence and less from a strictly logical analysis.

For more on the problems, controversies, and divisions around supervenience, mental causation, and emergence, see Clayton and Davies (2006); this discussion illustrates that these are far from settled issues. Nancey Murphy and Michael Silberstein are strong advocates for supervenience and mental causation. Jaejwon Kim is a fierce critic of those ideas. David Chalmers is, at best, an ambivalent supporter. In addition, both Silberstein and Chalmers critique traditional physicalism, and their arguments, along with Kim's, illustrate my main point in this chapter, that consciousness and mental causation cast serious doubts about any form of physicalism. For a fine, critical review of these debates see Tim Crane (1995 and 2003a). In these papers, Crane supports mental causation and is critical of the concept of supervenience. For another discussion supporting my main point here, see Tim Crane and D. H. Mellor (1990); that there is no question of physicalism is because physicalism is an indefensible philosophical position. Thus, one should be wary of relying on it in interpreting cognitive science and in fashioning antireligious polemics.

Dennis Bielfeldt's (1999a) paper covers much of the same ground. Bielfeldt draws on Kim's work more directly and his concerns are theologically focused on using downward causation to explain divine action rather than to account for research in self-regulation and behavioral medicine. Kim's (1998) treatment illustrates the way in which the argument about physicalism and mental causation depends upon certain rather robust models of causation. This raises the further question of whether such strong, virtually classical models of causation are compelling. Although he does not directly assert it, Silberstein (2001) implies that contemporary physics offers a rather different model of causation that might be relevant to the issue at hand. In Jones (1984), in an analysis of the theories of David Bohm, I also suggest a more open-textured model of causation. How such a newer model of causality might impact our understanding of mental causation and the relationship of consciousness and the brain is way beyond the scope of this chapter, except to say, with as much caution as possible, that such more current models of causality will probably not produce a view of the physical universe as inimical to a religious vision as did classical models of causation (Jones, 1984).

The sequence of observing one's own brain might be diagramed as follows, where NS stands for a neuronal state and CE stands for a conscious experience:

NS1 > CE1 (I see my brain)

[NS1 > CE1 (I see my brain)] > [NS2 > CE2 (I am aware that I am seeing my brain)]

{[NS1 > CE1 (I see my brain)] > [NS2 > CE2 (I am aware that I am seeing my brain)]} > {(NS3 > CE3 (I am aware that I am seeing my brain and the connection of that awareness to my brain)}

{[NS1 > CE1 (I see my brain)] > [NS2 > CE2 (I am aware that I am seeing my brain)]} > {(NS3 > CE3 (I am aware that I am seeing *my* brain and the connection of that awareness to my brain)} > NS4 > CE4 (I am aware that I am seeing my

brain and seeing the connection of that awareness to my
brain and seeing the connection of seeing that awareness
of my brain to my brain)]

This illustrates something of the complexity of self-reference and
self-reflexivity which is central to our experience of consciousness
and for which no current (2014) convincing philosophical or neurological accounts are even hypothetically available, despite extravagant claims to the contrary in the popular media.

A further critique of the assumptions on which the nonreductive physicalists appear to depend can be found in Nagel (1974); see
also Watkins (1982).

Philip Clayton (1999), while skeptical about nuancing or alter-
ing the idea of the closure of the physical world, writes "Science
does not need full determinism.... But it does need the world to
reflect at least patterns of probability over time" (p. 209). Everyone I read agrees that the world reflects "patterns of probability
over time" sufficient for scientific progress. Such "patterns of
probability" may not logically require the total causal closure of
the universe. In addition, Silberstein (2001, 2006) argues that
contemporary physics also suggests that the system of nature is
not causally closed in the rigid way classical physicalism claims.
During my year in Cambridge I had the privilege of discussing this
issue with George Ellis, who shared with me several, at the time,
unpublished papers on the topic, listed in the bibliography as Ellis
(2012, 2013).

The references to religious naturalism are from the following: Ursula Goodenough, *The Sacred Depths of Nature*
(New York: Oxford University Press, 1998): quotations are from
pages 174 (slightly altered), 102, 171; Wildman (2011): quotations are from pages 183, 262, 264; Robert Corrington, *Nature and
Spirit: An Essay in Ecstatic Naturalism* (New York: Fordham University Press, 1992): quotations are from pages x, xi, 32, 34; Rolston
(2006): quotations are from pages 64, 323, 303. Rolston's reference
to Eiseley is on page 133. The Eiseley quotation is from *The Immense
Journey* (New York: Vintage, 1957), page 210.

Chapter 5: Our Pluralistic Universe

The chapter title is taken from William James, whose book *A Pluralistic Universe* addresses many of the same issues mentioned in this chapter and comes to a similar conclusion.

Gould articulates his NOMA model in Gould (1999). Dawkins's rejection of this idea can be found in Dawkins (2006).

McCauley (2000) does not appear to me to be making this comparison in the hopes of debunking or eliminating religion. As a matter of fact, he says clearly that it is not a realistic goal, and he implies that wishing that science will eradicate or replace religion is more wishing than thinking. This article is a much more straightforward description of the differences between science and religion, and any suggestion that they perform similar explanatory functions pretty much drops out after the first few pages. Boyer, Bloom, Dennett, and Dawkins appear to ignore McCauley's description of differences between science and religion in order to argue that religion is a primitive science that must be replaced by modern science, an argument that makes sense only if religion and science are functionally similar.

My point about epistemic humility can be found in Jones (1981).

BIBLIOGRAPHY OF SOURCES

Alston, W. (1991). *Perceiving God.* Ithaca, NY: Cornell University Press.

Andresen, J. (2000). Meditation meets behavioural medicine: The story of experimental research on meditation. *Journal of Consciousness Studies,* 7(11–12), 17–74.

Atran, S. (2002). *In Gods we trust: The evolutionary landscape of religion.* Oxford: Oxford University Press.

Atran, S., & Henrich, J. (2010). The evolution of religion: How cognitive by-products, adaptive learning heuristics, ritual displays, and group competition generate deep commitments to prosocial relations. *Biological Theory,* 5(1), 1–30.

Austin, J. (1998). *Zen and the brain.* Cambridge: MIT Press.

Baldwin, M. W. (1992). Relational schemas and the processing of social information. *Psychological Bulletin,* 112(3), 461–484.

Barber, J. (1996). *Hypnosis and suggestion in the treatment of pain: A clinical guide.* New York: W. W. Norton.

Barnard, P. J., & Teasdale, J. D. (1991). Interacting cognitive subsystems: A systemic approach to cognitive-affective interaction and change. *Cognition and Emotion,* 5, 1–39.

Barrett, H. C., & Kurzban, R. (2006). Modularity in cognition. *Psychological Review,* 113(3), 628–647.

Barrett, J., & Zahl, B. (2013). Cognition, evolution, and religion. In K. Pargament, J, Exline, & J. Jones (Eds.), *APA handbook of psychology, religion, and spirituality,* (Vol. 1, pp. 221–238). Washington, DC: American Psychological Association.

Barrett, J. L. (1999). Theological correctness: Cognitive constraint and the study of religion. *Method and Theory in the Study of Religion,* 11, 325–339.

Barrett, J. L. (2001). How ordinary cognition informs petitionary prayer. *Journal of Cognition and Culture*, 1(3), 259–269.

Barrett, J. L. (2004). *Why would anyone believe in God?* Walnut Creek, CA: Altamira.

Barrett, J. L. (2007). Is the spell really broken? Bio-psychological explanations of religion and theistic belief. *Theology and Science*, 5(1), 57–72.

Barrett, J. L. (2008). Why Santa Claus is not a God. *Journal of Cognition and Culture*, 8(1–2), 149–161.

Barrett, J. L. (2010). The relative unnaturalness of atheism. *Religion*, 40(3), 169–172.

Barrett, J. L. (2011). Cognitive science of religion: Looking forward, looking backward. *Journal for the Scientific Study of Religion*, 50(2), 229–239.

Barrett, J. L., Burdett, E. R., & Porter, T. J. (2009). Counterintuitiveness in folktales: Finding the cognitive optimum. *Journal of Cognition and Culture*, 9(3), 271–287.

Barrett, J. L., & Keil, F. C. (1996). Anthropomorphism and God concepts: Conceptualizing a non-natural entity. *Cognitive Psychology*, 31, 219–247.

Barrett, J. L., Newman, R. M., & Richert, R. A. (2003). When seeing does not lead to believing: Children's understanding of the importance of background knowledge for interpreting visual displays. *Journal of Cognition and Culture*, 3(1), 91–108.

Barrett, J. L., & Nyhof, M. (2001). Spreading non-natural concepts: The role of intuitive conceptual structures in memory and transmission of cultural materials. *Journal of Cognition and Culture*, 1(1), 69–100.

Barrett, J. L., Richert, R. A., & Driesenga, A. (2001). God's beliefs versus Mom's: The development of natural and non-natural agent concepts. *Child Development*, 72(1), 50–65.

Barrett, N. F. (2010). Toward an alternative evolutionary theory of religion. Published with commentary and response. *Journal of the American Academy of Religion*, 78(3), 583–632.

Basmajian, J. V. (1983). *Biofeedback-principles and practices for clinicians*. Baltimore, MD: Williams & Wilkins.

Bering, J. M. (2002). Intuitive conceptions of dead agents' minds: The natural foundations of afterlife beliefs as phenomenological boundary. *Journal of Cognition and Culture*, 2, 263–308.

Bering, J. M. (2003). Towards a cognitive theory of existential meaning. *New Ideas in Psychology* 21, 101–120.

Bering, J. M. (2006). The folk psychology of souls. *Behavioral and Brain Sciences*, 29, 453–462.

Bering, J. M., & Bjorkland. D. F. (2004). The natural emergence of reasoning about the afterlife as a developmental regularity. *Developmental Psychology* 40, 217–233.

Bering, J. M., Hernández-Blasi, C., & Bjorkland, D. F. (2005). The development of "afterlife" beliefs in secularly and religiously schooled children. *British Journal of Developmental Psychology*, 23, 587–607.

Bering, J. M., & Johnson. D. D. P. (2005). "O Lord . . . You perceive my thoughts from afar": Recursiveness and the evolution of supernatural agency. *Journal of Cognition and Culture*, 5, 118–142.

Bielfeldt, D. (1999a). Can downward causation make the mental matter? A reply to Meyering and Murphy. *CTNS Bulletin*, 19(4), 11–21.

Bielfeldt, D. (1999b). Nancey Murphy's nonreductive physicalism. *Zygon*, 34(4), 619–628.

Bielfeldt, D. (2001). Can Western monotheism avoid substance dualism? *Zygon*, 36(1), 153–177.

Bloom, P. (2005). Is God an accident? *Atlantic Unbound*, December 2005.

Bloom, P. (2007). Religion is natural. *Developmental Science*, 10, 147–151.

Bloom, P. (Ed.). (2009). *Religious belief as an evolutionary accident*. New York: Oxford University Press.

Boyer, P. (1996). What makes anthropomorphism natural: Intuitive ontology and cultural representations. *Journal of the Royal Anthropological Institute*, 2, 83–97.

Boyer, P. (2001). *Religion explained: The evolutionary origins of religious thought*. New York: Basic Books.

Boyer, P. (2003). Religious thought and behavior as by-products of brain function. *Trends in Cognitive Sciences*, 7, 119–124.

Boyer, P. (2008). Religion: Bound to believe? *Nature*, 455, 1038–1039.

Boyer, P., & Lienard, P. (2006). Why ritualized behavior? *Behavioral and Brain Sciences*, 29(6), 1–56.

Boyer, P., & Ramble, C. (2001). Cognitive templates for religious concepts: Cross-cultural evidence for recall of counter-intuitive representations. *Cognitive Science*, 25, 535–564.

Brown, D., & Fromm, E. (1987). *Hypnosis and behavioral medicine.* Hillsdale, NJ: Erlbaum.

Brown, W, Murphy, N., & Malony, N. (Eds.). (1998). *Whatever happened to the soul?* Minneapolis, MN: Fortress.

Bulbulia, J. (2009). Charismatic signaling. *Journal of Religion and Culture,* 3(4), 518–551.

Bulkeley, K. (Ed.). (2005). *The wondering brain: Thinking about religion with and beyond cognitive neuroscience.* New York: Routledge.

Carlson, L., Speca, M, Petal, K., & Goodey, E. (2003). Mindfulness-based stress reduction in relation to quality of life, mood, symptoms of stress, and immune parameters in breast and prostate cancer outpatients. *Psychosomatic Medicine,* 65, 571–581.

Carruthers, P. (2006). *The architecture of the mind.* Oxford: Clarendon Press.

Chalmers, D. (1995). Facing up to the problem of consciousness. *Journal of Consciousness Studies,* 2(3), 200–219.

Clark, K. J., & Barrett, J. L. (2010). Reformed epistemology and the cognitive science of religion. *Faith and Philosophy,* 27(2), 174–189.

Clark, K. J., & Barrett, J. L. (2011). Reidian religious epistemology and the cognitive science of religion. *Journal of the American Academy of Religion,* 79(3), 639–675.

Clayton, P. (1999). Neuroscience, the person, and God. In R. J. Russell, N. Murphy, T. C. Meyering, & M. M. Arbib (Eds.), *Neuroscience and the person: Scientific perspectives on divine action* (pp. 181–214). Notre Dame, IN: University of Notre Dame Press.

Clayton, P., & Davies, P. (2006). *The re-emergence of emergence.* New York: Oxford.

Cohen, E., & Barrett, J. L. (2008). When minds migrate: Conceptualizing spirit possession. *Journal of Cognition and Culture,* 8(1–2), 23–48.

Cowie, F. (2008). Us, them and it. *Mind & Language,* 23(3), 284–292.

Crane, T. (1995). The mental causation debate. *Proceedings of the Aristotelian Society Supplementary Volume* 69, 1–23.

Crane, T. (2003a). Mental substances. *Royal Institute of Philosophy Supplement, Minds and Persons,* 53, 229–250.

Crane, T. (2003b). The significance of emergence. In B. Loewer & G. Gillet (Eds.), *Physicalism and its discontents* (pp. 207–224). Cambridge: Cambridge University Press.

Crane, T., & Mellor, D. H. (1990). There is no question of physicalism. *Mind*, 99, 394–418.

Davidson, R., Kabat-Zinn, J., Shumacher, J., Rosenkranz, M., Muller, D., Santorelli, S., . . . & Sheridan, J. (2003). Alterations in brain and immune function produced by mindfulness meditation. *Psychosomatic Medicine*, 65, 564–570.

Dawkins, R. (2006). *The God delusion*. London: Bantam.

Day, M. (2004). Religion, off-line cognition and the extended mind. *Journal of Cognition and Culture*, 4(1), 101–121.

Day, M. (2007). Let's be realistic: Evolutionary complexity, epistemic probabilism, and the cognitive science of religion. *Harvard Theological Review*, 100(1), 47–74.

Deikman, A. (2000). A functional approach to mysticism. *Journal of Consciousness Studies*, 7(11–12), 75–92.

Dennett, D. (2006). *Breaking the spell: Religion as a natural phenomenon*. New York: Viking.

Descombes, V. (2001). *The mind's provisions*. Trans. S. A. Schwartz. Princeton, NJ: Princeton University Press.

DuBreuil, S., & Spamos, N. (1993). Psychological treatment of warts. In J. Rhue, S. Lynn, & I. Kirsh (Eds.). *Handbook of clinical hypnosis* (pp. 623–648). Washington, DC: American Psychological Association.

Eccles, J. (Ed.). (1982). *Mind and brain: The many-faceted problems*. New York: Paragon.

Ellis, G. F. R. (2012). On the limits of quantum theory: Contextuality and the quantum-classical cut. Unpublished text.

Ellis, G. F. R. (2013). The functioning of complex systems: How can physics underlie the human mind? Unpublished text.

Evans, E. M. (2001). Cognitive and contextual factors in the emergence of diverse belief systems: Creation versus evolution. *Cognitive Psychology*, 42, 217–266.

Fagen, B. (2010). *Cro-Magnon*. New York: Bloomsbury.

Feldman, J. (2004). The neurobiology of pain, affect, and hypnosis. *American Journal of Clinical Hypnosis*, 46, 187–200.

Fodor, J. (2001). *The mind doesn't work that way*. Cambridge, MA: MIT Press.

Forgas, J. P. (Ed.). (2001). *Handbook of affect and cognition*. Hillsdale, NJ: Lawrence Erlbaum.

Geertz, A. C., & Markússon, G. (2009). Religion is natural, atheism is not: On why everybody is both right and wrong. *Religion*, 40(3), 152–165.

Gelman, S. A., & Kremer. K. E. (1991). Understanding natural cause: Children's explanations of how objects and their properties originate. *Child Development*, 62, 396–414.

Gibbs, R. (2005). *Embodiment and cognitive science*. Cambridge: Cambridge University Press.

Gibson, N. J. S. (2007). Measurement issues in God image research and practice. In G. L. Moriarty & L. D. Hoffman (Eds.), *God image handbook for spiritual counseling and psychotherapy: Research, theory, and practice* (pp. 227–246). Binghamton, NY: Haworth.

Gibson, N. J. S. (2008). Once more with feelings: The importance of emotion for cognitive science of religion. In J. Bulbulia, R. Sosis, E. Harris, R. Genet, C. Genet, & K. Wyman (Eds.), *The evolution of religion: Studies, theories, and critiques* (pp. 271–277). Santa Margarita, CA: Collins Foundation.

Goldapple, K., Segal, Z., Garson, C., Lau, M., Bieling, P., Kennedy, S., & Mayberg, H. (2004). Modulation of cortical-limbic pathways in major depression. *Archives of General Psychiatry*, 61, 34–41.

Goleman, D. (2003). *Destructive emotions*. New York: Bantam.

Gould, S. J. (1999). *Rock of ages*. New York: Ballantine.

Green, E., & Green, A. (1977). *Beyond biofeedback*. New York: Delacorte.

Gregory, J., & Barrett, J. L. (2009). Epistemology and counter-intuitiveness: Role and relationship in epidemiology of cultural representation. *Journal of Cognition and Culture*, 9(3), 289–314.

Griffin, D. (1998). *Unsnarling the world knot: Consciousness, freedom and the mind-body problem*. Berkeley: University of California Press.

Griffin, D. (2002). Scientific naturalism, the mind-body relation, and religious experience. *Zygon*, 37, 361–380.

Guthrie, S. E. (1993). *Faces in the clouds: A new theory of religion*. New York: Oxford University Press.

Heider, F., & Simmel, M. (1944). An experimental study of apparent behavior. *American Journal of Psychology*, 57, 243–249.

Heil, J., & Mele, A. (1993). *Mental causation*. Oxford: Clarendon Press.

Hofstader, D. R., & Dennett, D. C. (Eds.). (1981). *The mind's I*. New York. Basic Books.

Hutto, D. (1998). An ideal solution to the problem of consciousness. *Journal of Consciousness Studies*, 5(3), 328–341.

Jones, J. (1981). *The texture of knowledge: An essay on religion and science*. Lanham, MD: University Press of America.

Jones, J. (1984). *The redemption of matter: Towards the rapprochement of science and religion*. Lanham, MD: University Press of America.

Jones, J. (1989). Personality and epistemology: Cognitive social learning theory as a philosophy of science. *Zygon*, 24(1), 23–38.

Jones, J. (1992). Can neuroscience provide a complete account of human nature? *Zygon*, 27(2), 187–202.

Jones, J. (2003a). *The mirror of God: Christian faith as spiritual practice*. New York: Palgrave.

Jones, J. (2003b). Brain, mind, and spirit—A clinician's perspective, or, Why I am not afraid of dualism. In K. Bulkeley (Ed.), *Soul, psyche, brain: New directions in the study of religion and brain-mind science* (pp. 36–60). New York: Palgrave.

Jones, J. (2004). Religion, health, and the psychology of religion: How the research on religion and health helps us understand religion. *Journal of Religion and Health*, 43(4), 317–328.

Jones, J. (2006). *Waking from Newton's sleep: Dialogues on spirituality in an age of science*. Eugene, OR: Wipf and Stock.

Kabat-Zinn, J. (1990). *Full catastrophe living*. New York: Delacorte.

Kahneman, D. (2003). A perspective on judgment and choice: Mapping bounded rationality. *American Psychologist*, 58(9), 697–720.

Kaufman, S. (1995). *At home in the Universe*. New York: Oxford University Press.

Kelemen, D. (1999a). The scope of teleological thinking in preschool children. *Cognition*, 70, 241–272.

Kelemen, D. (1999b). Why are rocks pointy? Children's preference for teleological explanations of the natural world. *Developmental Psychology*, 35, 1440–1453.

Kelemen, D. (2004). Are children "intuitive theists"? Reasoning about purpose and design in nature. *Psychological Science*, 15, 295–301.

Kelemen, D., & DiYanni, C. (2005). Intuitions about origins: Purpose and intelligent design in children's reasoning about nature. *Journal of Cognition & Development*, 6, 3–31.

Kelemen, D., & Rosset, E. (2009). The human function compunction: Teleological explanation in adults. *Cognition*, 111, 138–143.

Kihlstrom, J. (2002). The seductions of materialism and the pleasures of dualism. *Journal of Consciousness Studies*, 9(11), 30–34.

Kim, J. (1998). *Mind in a physical world.* Cambridge, MA: MIT Press.

Kosslyn, S. M., et al. (1993). Visual mental imagery activates topo-graphically organized visual cortex: PET investigations. *Journal of Cognitive Neuroscience* 5(3), 263–287.

Kristeller, J. L., & Hallett, B. (1999). Effects of a meditation-based intervention in the treatment of binge eating. *Journal of Health Psychology,* 4(3), 357–363.

Laidlaw, J. (2007). A well-disposed social anthropologist's problems with the cognitive science of religion. In H. Whitehouse & J. Laidlaw (Eds.), *Religion, anthropology and cognitive science* (pp. 211–245). Durham: University of North Carolina Press.

Lawson, E. T., & McCauley, R. N. (1990). *Rethinking religion: Connecting cognition and culture.* Cambridge: Cambridge University Press.

Lenderking, W. R., & Santorelli, S. F. (1992). Effectiveness of a meditation-based stress reduction program in the treatment of anxiety disorders. *American Journal of Psychology,* 149(7), 936–943.

Libet, B. (1967). Responses of human somatosensory cortex to stimuli below threshold for conscious experience. *Science,* 158, 1597–1600.

Libet, B. (1978). Neuronal versus subjective timing for a conscious sensory experience. In P. A. Buser & A. Rougeul-Buser (Eds.), *Cerebral correlates of conscious experience* (pp. 149–162). Amster-dam: North Holland Press.

Libet, B. (1982). Subjective and neuronal time factors in conscious sensory experience and their implications for the mind-brain relationship. In J. Eccles (Ed.), *Mind and brain: The many-faceted problems* (pp. 99–102). New York: Paragon.

Libet, B. (1996). Neural processes in conscious experience. In M. Velmans (Ed.), *The science of consciousness* (pp. 96–117). London: Routledge.

Lienard, P. & Boyer, P. (2006). Whence collective rituals? *American Anthropologist,* 108(4), 814–827.

Linden, D. (2006). How psychotherapy changes the brain. *Molecular Psychiatry* 11(6), 528–538.

Linehan, M. (1993). *Cognitive-behavioral treatment of borderline person-ality disorder.* New York: Guilford.

Machery, E. (2008). Massive modularity and the flexibility of human cognition. *Mind & Language,* 23(3), 263–272.

Mackie, J. L. (1982). *The miracle of theism*. Oxford: Oxford University Press.

Marlatt, G. A., & Kristeller, J. L. (1999). Mindfulness and meditation. In W. R. Miller (Ed.), *Integrating spirituality in treatment* (pp. 67–84). Washington, DC: American Psychological Association.

McCauley, R. (2000). The naturalness of religion and the unnaturalness of science. In F. Kiel & R. Wilson (Eds.), *Explanation and cognition* (pp. 61–85). Cambridge, MA: MIT Press.

McCauley, R. (2011). *Why religion is natural and science is not*. New York: Oxford University Press.

McCauley, R. N., & Lawson, E. T. (2002). *Bringing ritual to mind: Psychological foundations of cultural forms*. Cambridge: Cambridge University Press.

McGinn, C. (1989). Can we solve the mind-body problem? *Mind*, 88, 349–366.

Meyering, T. (1999). Mind matters, In R. J. Russell, N. Murphy, T. C. Mevering, & M. M. Arbib (Eds.), *Neuroscience and the person: Scientific perspectives on divine action* (pp. 165–180). Notre Dame, IN: University of Notre Dame Press.

Morowitz, H. J. (1981). Rediscovering the mind. In D. R. Hofstader and D. C. Dennett (Eds.), *The mind's I* (pp. 34–41). New York: Basic Books.

Murphy, N. (1998). Nonreductive physicalism: Philosophical issues. In W. Brown, N. Murphy, & H. N. Malony (Eds.), *Whatever happened to the soul? Scientific and theological portraits of human nature* (pp. 127–148). Minneapolis, MN: Fortress.

Murphy, N. (1999a). Supervenience and the downward efficacy of the mental: A nonreductive physicalist account of human action In R. J. Russell, N. Murphy, T. C. Meyering, & M. M. Arbib (Eds.), *Neuroscience and the person: Scientific perspectives on divine action* (pp. 147–164). Notre Dame, IN: University of Notre Dame Press.

Murphy, N. (1999b). Downward causation and why the mental matters. *CTNS Bulletin*, 19(1), 13–21.

Murphy, N. (1999c). Physicalism without reductionism: toward a scientifically, philosophically, and theologically sound portrait of human nature. *Zygon*, 34(4), 551–571.

Murray, M. J. (2008). Four arguments that the cognitive psychology of religion undermines the justification of religious beliefs. In

J. S. Bulbulia, R. Sosis, E. Harris, R. Genet, C. Genet, & K. Wyman (Eds.), *The evolution of religion: Studies, theories, and critiques* (pp. 365–370). Santa Margarita, CA: Collins Foundation.

Murray, M. J. (2009). Scientific explanations of religion and the justification of religious belief. In J. Schloss & M. Murray (Eds.), *The believing primate: Scientific, philosophical, and theological reflections on the origin of religion* (pp. 168–178). Oxford: Oxford University Press.

Murray, M. J., & Moore, L. (2009). Costly signaling and the origin of religion. *Journal of Cognition and Culture*, 9(3–4), 225–245.

National Geographic. (2011). The birth of religion, 219(6), June 2011, 34–59.

Nagel, T. (1974). What is it like to be a bat? *Philosophical Review*, 83, 435–450.

Nagel, T. (2012). *Mind and cosmos*. New York: Oxford University Press.

Oviedo, L. (2008). Is a complete biocognitive account of religion feasible? *Zygon*, 43(1), 101–126.

Penfield, W. (1975). *The mystery of the mind*. Princeton: Princeton University Press.

Popper, K., & Eccles, J. (1977). *The self and its brain*. New York: Springer International.

Poulton, E. P. (1973). *Critique of the psycho-physical identity theory*. The Hague: Mouton.

Preston, J., & Epley, N. (2005). Explanation versus application: The explanatory power of valuable beliefs. *Psychological Science*, 16(10), 826–832.

Proudfoot, W., & Shaver, P. (1975). Attribution theory and the psychology of religion. *Journal for the Scientific Study of Religion*, 14(4), 317–330.

Quine, W. V. O. (1951). Major trends in recent philosophy: Two dogmas of empiricism. *Philosophical Review*, 60(1), 20–43.

Raz, A., et al. (2007). Selective biasing of a specific bistable-figure percept involves fMRI signal changes in frontostriatal circuits: A step toward unlocking the neural correlates of top-down control and self-regulation. *American Journal of Clinical Hypnosis*, 50(2), 137–156.

Richert, R. A., & Barrett, J. L. (2005). Do you see what I see? Young children's assumptions about God's perceptual abilities. *International Journal for the Psychology of Religion*, 15, 283–295.

Robinson, D. M. (1982). Some thoughts on the matter of the mind/ body problem. In J. Eccles (Ed.), *Mind and brain: The many-faceted problems* (pp. 197–206). New York. Paragon.

Robinson, H. M. (1976). The mind-body problem in contemporary philosophy. *Zygon* 11, 346–360.

Robinson, M. (2010). *Absence of Mind*. New Haven, CT: Yale University Press.

Rolston, H. (2006). *Science and religion: A critical survey*. West Conshohocken, PA: Templeton Press.

Rurzyla-Smith, P., Barabasz, A., Barabasz, M., & Warner, D. (1995). Effects of hypnosis on immune response. *American Journal of Clinical Hypnosis*, 38, 71–79.

Russell, R. J., Murphy, N., Meyering, & Arbib, M. M. (1999). *Neuroscience and the person: Scientific perspectives on divine action*. Notre Dame, IN: Vatican Observatory Publications.

Schloss, J., & Murray, M. (Eds.). (2009). *The believing primate: Scientific, philosophical, and theological reflections on the origin of religion*. Oxford: Oxford University Press.

Schwartz, G., & Beatty, J. (1977). *Biofeedback theory and research*. New York: Academic.

Schwartz, J. (1999). A role for volition and attention in the generation of new brain circuitry. *Journal of Consciousness Studies*, 6(6–9), 115–142.

Scott, A. (2004). Reductionism revisited. *Journal of Consciousness Studies*, 11(2), 51–68.

Segal, Z., Williams, J., & Teasdale, J. (2002). *Mindfulness-based cognitive therapy for depression*. New York: Guilford.

Shapiro, S., Schwartz, G., & Bonner, G. (1998). Effects of mindfulness-based stress reduction on medical and premedical students. *Journal of Behavioral Medicine*, 21, 581–599.

Shariff, A. F., & Norenzayan, A. (2007). God is watching you: Priming God concepts increase prosocial behavior in an anonymous economic game. *Psychological Science*, 18(9), 803–809.

Sheikh, A., Kunzendorf, R., & Sheikh, K. (1996). Somatic consequences of consciousness. In M. Velmans (Ed.), *The science of consciousness* (pp. 140–161). London: Routledge.

Silberstein, M. (2001). Converging on emergence: Consciousness, causation, and explanation. *Journal of Consciousness Studies*, 8(9–10), 61–98.

Silberstein, M. (2006). In defence of mental causation and ontological emergence. In P. Clayton & P. Davies (Eds.), *The re-emergence of emergence* (pp. 203–226). New York: Oxford.

Slingerland, E. (2008a). *What science offers the humanities.* Cambridge: Cambridge University Press.

Slingerland, E. (2008b). Who's afraid of reductionism? The study of religion in the age of cognitive science [with commentaries and response]. *Journal of the American Academy of Religion*, 76(2), 375–456.

Slone, D. J. (2004). *Theological incorrectness: Why religious people believe what they shouldn't.* New York: Oxford University Press.

Smith, B. H. (2006). *Scandalous knowledge.* Durham, NC: Duke University Press.

Smith, B. H. (2010). *Natural reflections: Human cognition at the nexus of science and religion.* New Haven, CT: Yale University Press.

Sosis, R. (2004). The adaptive value of religious ritual: Rituals promote group cohesion by requiring members to engage in behavior that is too costly to fake. *American Scientists*, 92, 166–174.

Sosis, R., & Bressler, E. (2003). Cooperation and commune longevity: A test of the costly signaling theory of religion. *Cross-Cultural Research*, 37, 211–239.

Sperry, R. W. (1991). Search for beliefs to live by consistent with science. *Zygon*, 26, 237–258.

Spilka, B., Shaver, P. R., & Kirkpatrick, L. A. (1985). A general attribution theory for the psychology of religion. *Journal for the Scientific Study of Religion*, 24(1), 1–20.

Stanford, K. (2011). Damn the consequences: Projective evidence and the heterogeneity of scientific explanation. *Philosophy of Science*, 78(5), 887–899.

Taves, A. (2009). *Religious experience reconsidered.* Princeton, NJ: Princeton University Press.

Teske, J. (2013). From embodied to extended cognition. *Zygon*, 48(3), 759–781.

Thagard, P. (2005). The emotional coherence of religion. *Journal of Cognition and Culture*, 5(1–2), 58–74.

Toulmin, S. (1960). *The philosophy of science.* New York: Harper & Row.

Turner, L. (2014). Introduction: Pluralism and complexity in evolutionary cognitive science of religion, In F. N. Watts & L. Turner (Eds.), *Evolution, religion and cognitive science* (pp. 1–21). Oxford: Oxford University Press.

Van Gulick, R. (1993). Who's in charge here? And who's doing all the work? In J. Heil & A. Mele (Eds.), *Mental causation* (pp. 233–257). Oxford: Clarendon Press.

Velmans, M. (Ed.). (1996). *The science of consciousness*. London: Routledge.

Velmans, M. (2000). *Understanding consciousness*. London: Routledge.

Velmans, M. (2002). How could conscious experiences affect brains? *Journal of Consciousness Studies*, 9(11), 3–29.

Wallace, B. A. (2012). *Meditations of a Buddhist skeptic: A manifesto for the mind sciences and contemplative practices*. New York: Columbia University Press.

Watkins, J. (1982). A basic difficulty in the mind-brain identity hypothesis. In J. Eccles (Ed.), *Mind and brain: The many-faceted problems* (pp. 221–232). New York: Paragon.

Watts, F. N. (1996). Psychological and religious perspectives on emotion. *International Journal for the Psychology of Religion*, 6(2), 71–87.

Watts, F. N. (2002). *Theology and psychology*. Aldershot, UK: Ashgate.

Watts, F. N. (2006). Implicational and propositional religious meanings. Unpublished manuscript, University of Cambridge, UK.

Watts, F. N., & Turner, L. (Eds.). (2014). *Evolution, religion, and cognitive science*. Oxford: Oxford University Press.

Watts, F. N., & Williams, M. (1988). *The psychology of religious knowing*. Cambridge: Cambridge University Press.

Whitehouse, H. (2002). Modes of religiosity: Towards a cognitive explanation of the sociopolitical dynamics of religion. *Mind & Theory in the Study of Religion*, 14, 293–315.

Whitehouse, H. (2007). Towards an integration of ethnography, history, and the cognitive science of religion. In H. Whitehouse & J. Laidlaw (Eds.), *Religion, anthropology and cognitive science* (pp. 247–280). Durham: University of North Carolina Press.

Whitehouse, H. (2008). Cognitive evolution and religion; *Cognition and Religious Evolution: Issues in Ethnology and Anthropology*, 3(3), 35–47.

Whitehouse, H., & Laidlaw, J. (2007). *Religion, anthropology and cognitive science*. Durham, NC: University of North Carolina Press.

Wildman, W. (2011). *Religious and spiritual experiences*. Cambridge: Cambridge University Press.

Wilford, J. N. (2012). With science, new portrait of the cave artist. *New York Times,* June 14.

Wilson, D. S. (2002). *Darwin's cathedral: Evolution, religion, and the nature of society.* Chicago: University of Chicago Press.

Wood, G., Bughi, S., Morrison, J., Tanavoli, S., Tanavoli, S., & Zadeh, H. (2003). Hypnosis, differential expression cytokines by T-cell subsets, and the hypothalamo-pituitary axis. *American Journal of Clinical Hypnosis,* 45, 179–193.

Woody, E., & Szechtman, H. (2000). Hypnotic hallucinations: Towards a biology of epistemology. *Contemporary Hypnosis,* 17(1), 4–14.

INDEX